OPPOSING VIEWPOINTS® SERIES

Terrorism

DISCARD

DATE DUE

October 14, 2009	
OCT 3 1 2010	

BRODART, CO.   Cat. No. 23-221

Other Books of Related Interest:

Opposing Viewpoints Series

America's Global Influence

Bioterrorism

Cyber Crime

National Security

Nation-Building

Rogue Nations

Current Controversies

Homeland Security

The Middle East

Weapons of Mass Destruction

At Issue Series

Can the War on Terrorism Be Won?

National Security

Should Governments Negotiate with Terrorists?

"Congress shall make
no law . . . abridging
the freedom of speech,
or of the press."

First Amendment to the U.S. Constitution

The basic foundation of our democracy is the First Amendment guarantee of freedom of expression. The *Opposing Viewpoints* Series is dedicated to the concept of this basic freedom and the idea that it is more important to practice it than to enshrine it.

Terrorism

Mike Wilson, Book Editor

GREENHAVEN PRESS
A part of Gale, Cengage Learning

GALE
CENGAGE Learning

Detroit • New York • San Francisco • New Haven, Conn • Waterville, Maine • London

Christine Nasso, *Publisher*
Elizabeth Des Chenes, *Managing Editor*

© 2009 Greenhaven Press, a part of Gale, Cengage Learning

Gale and Greenhaven Press are registered trademarks used herein under license.

For more information, contact:
Greenhaven Press
27500 Drake Rd.
Farmington Hills, MI 48331-3535
Or you can visit our Internet site at gale.cengage.com

For product information and technology assistance, contact us at

Gale Customer Support, 1-800-877-4253
For permission to use material from this text or product, submit all requests online at www.cengage.com/permissions

Further permissions questions can be emailed to permissionrequest@cengage.com

Articles in Greenhaven Press anthologies are often edited for length to meet page requirements. In addition, original titles of these works are changed to clearly present the main thesis and to explicitly indicate the author's opinion. Every effort is made to ensure that Greenhaven Press accurately reflects the original intent of the authors. Every effort has been made to trace the owners of copyrighted material.

Cover image © Mark Plumley, 2008. Used under license from Shutterstock.com.

LIBRARY OF CONGRESS CATALOGING-IN-PUBLICATION DATA

Terrorism / Mike Wilson, book editor.
    p. cm. -- (Opposing viewpoints)
    Includes bibliographical references and index.
    ISBN 978-0-7377-4234-3 (hardcover)
    ISBN 978-0-7377-4235-0 (pbk.)
    1. Terrorism. I. Wilson, Mike, 1954-
    HV6431.T4576 2009
    363.325--dc22

                                                2008029140

Printed in the United States of America
1 2 3 4 5 6 7 12 11 10 09 08

Contents

Why Consider Opposing Viewpoints?

> "The only way in which a human being can make some approach to knowing the whole of a subject is by hearing what can be said about it by persons of every variety of opinion and studying all modes in which it can be looked at by every character of mind. No wise man ever acquired his wisdom in any mode but this."
>
> *John Stuart Mill*

In our media-intensive culture it is not difficult to find differing opinions. Thousands of newspapers and magazines and dozens of radio and television talk shows resound with differing points of view. The difficulty lies in deciding which opinion to agree with and which "experts" seem the most credible. The more inundated we become with differing opinions and claims, the more essential it is to hone critical reading and thinking skills to evaluate these ideas. *Opposing Viewpoints* books address this problem directly by presenting stimulating debates that can be used to enhance and teach these skills. The varied opinions contained in each book examine many different aspects of a single issue. While examining these conveniently edited opposing views, readers can develop critical thinking skills such as the ability to compare and contrast authors' credibility, facts, argumentation styles, use of persuasive techniques, and other stylistic tools. In short, the *Opposing Viewpoints* series is an ideal way to attain the higher-level thinking and reading skills so essential in a culture of diverse and contradictory opinions.

In addition to providing a tool for critical thinking, *Opposing Viewpoints* books challenge readers to question their own strongly held opinions and assumptions. Most people form their opinions on the basis of upbringing, peer pressure, and personal, cultural, or professional bias. By reading carefully balanced opposing views, readers must directly confront new ideas as well as the opinions of those with whom they disagree. This is not to simplistically argue that everyone who reads opposing views will—or should—change his or her opinion. Instead, the series enhances readers' understanding of their own views by encouraging confrontation with opposing ideas. Careful examination of others' views can lead to the readers' understanding of the logical inconsistencies in their own opinions, perspective on why they hold an opinion, and the consideration of the possibility that their opinion requires further evaluation.

Evaluating Other Opinions

To ensure that this type of examination occurs, *Opposing Viewpoints* books present all types of opinions. Prominent spokespeople on different sides of each issue as well as well-known professionals from many disciplines challenge the reader. An additional goal of the series is to provide a forum for other, less known, or even unpopular viewpoints. The opinion of an ordinary person who has had to make the decision to cut off life support from a terminally ill relative, for example, may be just as valuable and provide just as much insight as a medical ethicist's professional opinion. The editors have two additional purposes in including these less known views. One, the editors encourage readers to respect others' opinions—even when not enhanced by professional credibility. It is only by reading or listening to and objectively evaluating others' ideas that one can determine whether they are worthy of consideration. Two, the inclusion of such viewpoints encourages the important critical thinking skill of objectively evaluating an author's credentials and bias. This evaluation will illuminate an author's reasons for taking a particular stance on an issue and will aid in readers' evaluation of the author's ideas.

It is our hope that these books will give readers a deeper understanding of the issues debated and an appreciation of the complexity of even seemingly simple issues when good and honest people disagree. This awareness is particularly important in a democratic society such as ours in which people enter into public debate to determine the common good. Those with whom one disagrees should not be regarded as enemies but rather as people whose views deserve careful examination and may shed light on one's own.

Thomas Jefferson once said that "difference of opinion leads to inquiry, and inquiry to truth." Jefferson, a broadly educated man, argued that "if a nation expects to be ignorant and free. . .it expects what never was and never will be." As individuals and as a nation, it is imperative that we consider the opinions of others and examine them with skill and discernment. The *Opposing Viewpoints* series is intended to help readers achieve this goal.

David L. Bender and Bruno Leone,
Founders

Introduction

> *The term "international terrorism" means activities that (a) involve violent acts or acts dangerous to human life that are a violation of the criminal laws ... [and] (b) appear to be intended—*
>
> *(i) to intimidate or coerce a civilian population;*
>
> *(ii) to influence the policy of a government by intimidation or coercion; or*
>
> *(iii) to affect the conduct of a government by mass destruction, assassination or kidnapping. ...*
>
> —*U.S. Code Title 18, Section 2331*

The legal definition of terrorism quoted above applies to terrorism that occurs outside the United States or crosses national boundaries. A similar definition of "domestic terrorism" appears in the same section of the law for acts occurring in the United States. Although the law cited above is relatively new, terrorism has been employed as a method of warfare, by both small groups and nation-states, for centuries.

There are many examples in the Old Testament of the killing of women and children and the complete destruction of tribes or certain ethnic groups. Throughout history, however, this sort of brutality was not unusual and would not even be considered terrorism. The late political scientist Hans J. Morgenthau observed that "from the beginning of history through the better part of the Middle Ages, belligerents were held to be free, according to ethics as well as law, to kill all enemies whether or not they were members of the armed forces, or else to treat them in any way they saw fit. Men, women, and children were often put to the sword or sold into slavery by the victor without any adverse moral reactions taking place." In those times, Morgenthau noted, war was considered a contest between all the inhabitants of the territories of the belligerent states. The enemy to be fought included not only the armed forces of a nation or feudal state but also the individuals owing allegiance to a certain lord or living within a certain territory. Thus every individual citizen of the enemy state became an enemy of every individual citizen of the other party in the conflict.

In the West, after the end of the Thirty Years' War in Europe (1618-1648), the idea of war began to change. Over time, according to Morgenthau, "the distinction between combatants and noncombatants has become one of the fundamental legal and moral principles governing the actions of belligerents. War is considered to be a contest between the armed forces of the belligerent states, and, since the civilian populations do not participate actively in the armed contest, they are not to be made its object." International conventions, such as the Geneva Convention of 1949, recognize a legal and moral duty not to harm noncombatant civilians purposely. Although civilian injuries and deaths do occur during warfare, there is a duty to avoid them to the utmost.

But international laws and norms are not always followed, and nation-states continue to employ terrorism as an instrument of warfare or political control. To give only a few examples, Adolf Hitler, Joseph Stalin, Pol Pot, Saddam Hussein, and countless other dictators and warlords have employed terrorism. When British political and military leaders during World War II devised the strategy of bombing Germany's cities and towns, they themselves called it "terror bombing." The United States, too, has been labeled by some as employing terrorism during World War II by dropping the atom bomb on Nagasaki and Hiroshima, Japan, killing thousands of civilians.

However, most people today think of nonstate actors when they think of terrorism. This type of terrorism has also been around for centuries. Religious sects were among the earliest terrorists. The Sicari were Jewish zealots who murdered other Jews that collaborated with the Roman occupation during the first century C.E. Another group, the Assassins (from which the word "assassin" is derived), were an eleventh-century offshoot of the Ishmaili sect of Shiite Muslims. They murdered political foes and viewed their own deaths as martyrdoms.

Some would classify as terrorism the 1605 Guy Fawkes conspiracy to kill the king of England and members of Parliament by detonating gunpowder in the building where they were gathered. During the French Revolution, the phrase *regime de la terreur* (from which the word *terrorism* is derived) was coined to describe the estimated forty thousand people executed at the direction of the French revolutionary leader Maximilien Robespierre.

Igor Primoratz, professor emeritus of philosophy at Hebrew University in Jerusalem, writes in the *Cardoza Law Review* that an indiscriminate kind of terrorism emerged during the first quarter of the twentieth century in Russia. While early revolutionary groups in the country, he states, targeted individuals responsible for perceived injustices and attempted "to induce terror and force political change by assassinating royalty and holders of high government office," later revolutionaries engaged in indiscriminate killing, maiming, and destruction. "Lethal violence," notes Primoratz, "was no longer restricted to those whose deliberate actions had seriously implicated them in the tyranny that had to be overthrown, and whose execution could accordingly be seen not only as a useful means to the revolutionary cause, but also as deserved and just punishment." In other words, if the terrorist act would help achieve victory, the act was justified even if, according to Primoratz, "all or most of the victims of a terrorist attack would be innocent of whatever wrongs the terrorists were fighting against."

During the nineteenth and twentieth centuries, both targeted and indiscriminate methods of terrorism were employed for political purposes. In the United States, the Ku Klux Klan and similar groups terrorized black Americans by lynching, arson, and other means. During the 1930s and 1940s, a clandestine Zionist group known as Irgun conducted terrorist attacks against both Palestinian Arabs and the British who were then occupying Palestine. Throughout the 1960s and 1970s, various nationalist, ethnic, and ideological groups have turned to terrorism in order to achieve their aims. Groups accused of being terrorists included the Palestine Liberation Organization (PLO), the Basque ETA (Euskadi Ta Askatasuna), the Provisional Irish Republican Army (IRA), the Red Army Faction (in what was then West Germany), the Italian Red Brigades, and, in the United States, the Weathermen and Black Panthers.

During this period, Palestinian terrorists garnered the most attention by hijacking planes and, at the 1972 Olympic Games in Munich, Germany, seizing and murdering eleven Israeli athletes. During the 1990s, terrorist groups included the Colombian FARC (Revolutionary Armed Forces of Colombia), al Qaeda, and Japan's Aum Shinrikyo. In the United States, Terry McVeigh's bombing of the Alfred P. Murrah Federal Building in Oklahoma City in 1995 killed 168 people and injured more than 800—the worst terrorist incident in America prior to 9/11.

In the twenty-first century, terrorism by militant Islamic groups garners the most attention in the West and is the context for many articles in this collection. The authors present a range of opinions, providing context for the current debate surrounding terrorism. In *Opposing Viewpoints: Terrorism*, contributors discuss terrorism in the following chapters: Is Terrorism a Serious Threat? How Is Society Susceptible to Terrorism? What Causes Terrorism? How Should Governments Respond to Terrorism?

OPPOSING
VIEWPOINTS®
SERIES

CHAPTER 1

Is Terrorism a Serious Threat?

Chapter Preface

A 2003 poll found that 73 percent of Americans who were not direct victims of the 9/11 terrorist attacks felt that the events had changed them or their outlook on life. Clearly, terrorist acts have the power to impact not only those who are killed or wounded but an entire nation. Rand Corporation analysts Teri L. Tanielian and Bradley D. Stein point out in their book *Emergency Management, Public Health and Medical Preparedness* that "beyond the physical damage caused by the event itself, terrorism is intended to have a psychological effect. It targets the social capital of a nation—cohesion, values, and ability to function."

Terrorism can subvert the sense of community that holds a nation together. Former British prime minister Tony Blair, speaking to the U.S. Congress in 2003, stated that "the purpose of terrorism is not the single act of wanton destruction, it is the reaction it seeks to provoke: economic collapse, the backlash, the hatred, the division, the elimination of tolerance, until societies cease to reconcile their differences and become defined by them." Indeed, the September 11 terrorist attacks had an impact on many Muslim Americans. The Federal Bureau of Investigation (FBI) reported a 1500 percent increase in hate crimes against Muslim Americans during 2001. A 2002 Hamilton College poll of American Muslims found that over half reported they personally knew individuals who had been victims of anti-Muslim discrimination, harassment, or physical attack since 9/11. One in four said that they themselves had been victims of anti-Muslim discrimination, harassment, or attack in recent months.

In addition, terrorism often has an economic impact. The attacks of 9/11 caused property destruction estimated at $33 to $36 billion—a little more than 0.3 percent of U.S. gross domestic product that year. But it is the indirect cost of "fighting terrorism" that probably has the greatest effect on the U.S. economy. Economist David Gold, writing in the *Quarterly Journal*, observes, "Fighting terrorism requires resources, so there is an immediate economic cost that terrorism imposes. Businesses are forced to allocate more resources to security as the threat of terrorism increases." Companies that supply security services may have an increase in business, but this diverts resources from more productive activities.

Government spending to fight terrorism is another cost. The Department of Homeland Security (DHS) and other agencies spend billions fighting terrorism each year. The invasions of Afghanistan and Iraq that followed 9/11 were, according to U.S. leaders, necessary to fight the war on terrorism. The Congressional Budget Office (CBO) estimated in February 2007 that total government expenditures to fight terrorism since 2001 had totaled $746 billion.

Terrorists are aware of the economic costs they inflict. In 2004, al Qaeda leader Osama bin Laden issued a message to the American people vowing to wage a war of "attrition" against the United States until it is "bankrupt."

Terrorism also has an effect on freedom. After 9/11, Congress passed the so-called Patriot Act and other laws, which many people, especially civil libertarians, claim have compromised our constitutional rights and freedoms. The National Security Letter (NSL) provision of the Patriot Act expanded the FBI's authority to demand personal customer records from Internet service providers (such as the Web sites one visits and e-mail addresses with whom one corresponds), financial institutions, and credit companies without prior court approval. According to a Justice Department inspector general's report, between 2003 and 2006 the FBI issued nearly two hundred thousand NSLs. The American Civil Liberties Union reports that nearly one million people are on the U.S. "terrorist watch list," which is used by government agencies to check people seeking visas, visitors entering or leaving the country, passengers boarding domestic flights, and persons stopped by state, local, or federal law enforcement officers.

The viewpoints in the following chapter debate the success of America's war on terrorism.

> "At a time when we should be well into
> our planning for a long conflict, our
> attention is drifting form the greatest
> threat we face."

Terrorism Is a Serious Threat

Daniel Benjamin and Steven Simon

In the following viewpoint, Daniel Benjamin and Steven Simon argue that America has grown complacent since the attacks of 9/11 and no longer sees terrorism as an urgent problem or attacks on America as a real possibility. Although terrorist activity has increased, the focus on security issues has shifted to China, the authors maintain, while bureaucratic changes, such as reorganization of the nation's security and intelligence agencies, have wasted valuable time. The authors also argue that the Iraq war has provided terrorists a sanctuary and training ground and bolstered the view that the United States seeks to oppress Muslims. Daniel Benjamin is a senior fellow at the Center for Strategic and International Studies in Washington, D.C., and Steven Simon teaches at Georgetown University. They are authors of a book on terrorism, The Next Attack: The Failure of the War on Terror and a Strategy for Getting It Right, *from which the following viewpoint is taken.*

As you read, consider the following questions:

1. What has the war in Iraq given terrorists that, according to the authors, they most desired?
2. What terrorist incident do the authors say was likely incited by American and British presence in Iraq?
3. In the view of the authors, how did the sense of urgency expressed by President George W. Bush about terrorism change after the 2004 elections?

We are losing.

Four years and two wars after the attacks of September 11, 2001, America is heading for a repeat of the events of that day, or perhaps something worse. Against our most dangerous foe, our strategic position is weakening. Inspired by Usama bin Laden's boldness and outraged by America's recent actions, more Muslims are sympathizing with the radical Islamists and joining their movement. Individuals who hitherto had no significant ties to radical organizations are enlisting themselves in the struggle and committing acts of violence, sometimes without any support from existing networks. In disparate places around the globe, from Indonesia to the Caucasus and from Pakistan to Western Europe, the jihadist ideology has become the banner under which an array of grievances is being expressed, and often that expression is violent. In many of these regions, local and global grievances are merging into a pervasive hatred of the United States, its allies, and the international order they uphold. Within parts of the Muslim world, social and religious inhibitions on violence are weakening, and the notion is gaining acceptance that an attack on infidels involving weapons of mass destruction would be justified.

The United States—and certainly its leadership—appears not to have comprehended the dynamic, ideologically driven insurgency whose heralds were four hijacked commercial jets. Instead of taking a comprehensive view of the phenomenon of radical Islam, only two indicators are used to show the measure of our progress in the war on terror: the number of days since 9/11 in which we have not experienced a second catastrophic attack, and the number of al Qaeda members who have been apprehended or killed. While it is true that bin Laden's group has been seriously hurt by the capture of many of its leaders and the disruption of many of its cells, the administration's focus on numbers feeds the widespread belief that the terrorist enemy is finite in quantity and destructible in the near term. The failure to look beyond al Qaeda and to recognize the multiplying forms that the jihadist threat is taking represents a serious failure of vision. We are repeating the errors of the time before 9/11 in believing, first, that what terrorists do abroad has little consequence for national security, and, second, that only states can truly threaten us. Unwittingly, we are clearing the way for the next attack—and those that will come after.

Not only are we not attending to a growing threat, we are stoking the fire. America's invasion of Iraq has turned that long-suffering country into the central theater of the jihadist struggle. We destroyed one of the hated secular dictatorships of the Arab world that jihadists had been unable to dent but left an open field for radicals from outside the country and within to cause havoc. The terrorists have found in Iraq a better sanctuary, training ground, and laboratory than they ever had in Afghanistan. They have also been given what they desire most: American targets in close proximity. They can now demonstrate their valor and resolve to bleed America, and in doing so, to build momentum for their cause. We have slain the chimera of Saddam Hussein's Iraq, but we are nourishing the all-too-real dragon of radical Islam.

It is unlikely that even in his most feverish reveries, Usama bin Laden could have imagined that America would stumble so badly and wound itself so grievously. By occupying Iraq, the United States has played into the hands of its opponents, affirming the story they have been telling to the Muslim world and adding to their aura as true warriors in defense of Islam. America's image in the Muslim world has never been more battered, and the jihadist claim that the United States seeks to oppress Muslims has never seemed more plausible—no matter how noble we view our own sacrifices in the liberation of Iraq. There is, as has so often been said, a war of ideas going on, a battle for hearts and minds. Unfortunately, America has wound up on the wrong side.

We and our friends are paying a price for these errors. As this is being written, investigators are pursuing leads from the British Isles to Pakistan in connection with the July 7 [2005] bombing of three Underground trains in London and a double-decker bus. The attacks, carried out with the al Qaeda hallmark of multiple simultaneous blasts, appear to have been the work of three Britons of Pakistani descent and a Jamaican immigrant who had converted to Islam. It is not clear yet whether, as alleged, they benefited from bomb-making instruction in a jihadist training camp in Pakistan, but that is entirely plausible. Nor do we know what was going through their minds when they planned the incident that killed fifty-six people. But if they are anything like other recent terrorists, then their anger was fired by the presence of Americans, Britons, and others in Iraq. "Our military is confronting the terrorists, along with our allies, in Iraq and Afghanistan so that innocent civilians will not have to confront terrorist violence in Washington or London or anywhere else in the world," Vice President Dick Cheney said in September 2003. It has not turned out that way.

We have compounded these mistakes by squandering the chance to build defenses against a new kind of enemy. The

Findings of the Homeland Security Advisory Council, 2007

The most significant terrorist threat to the homeland today stems from a global movement, underpinned by a jihadist/Salafist ideology. [Salafism encourages the teaching of Islam that strictly follows a few commands and practices.] The members of this movement seek to overturn regimes considered to be apostate; to re-establish the Caliphate [the rulership of Islam] and to impose an extremist, militant interpretation of Islam. Some have cast the struggle within the Muslim world over interpretation of the Qur'an as a battle for the "soul of Islam." Other extremists have grievances and aims that are more localized.

The core of al Qaeda is resilient and resurgent, and remains a threat to the United States. We cannot dismiss the possibility that this group, operating out of safe havens in Pakistan and elsewhere, will succeed in executing large-scale, spectacular, mass casualty attacks against the United States and our interests abroad. However, "al Qaeda Classic" is a degraded entity with many of its remaining key figures on the run.

Looking to the future, a more pressing threat will be the wider movement spawned by al Qaeda and inspired and motivated by its ideology. Al Qaeda has franchised itself across the globe, with its franchises prepared to act locally, and largely independently—in effect a network of networks. Attacks on the United States, its interests, and its allies, are seen as a means to accomplish these ends. We have seen the recent emergence of a leaderless movement, marked significantly by self enlistments, to include "homegrown" terrorists taking its inspiration from "al Qaeda Classic" to join the global Salafi jihad, or to act on more local grievances.

Homeland Security Advisory Council,
Report on the Future of Terrorism, *January 2007.*

successes we have notched against the leadership of al Qaeda have bought us time, but the time has been wasted. When American political leaders wish to show seriousness they first declare war on a problem, then they decree a bureaucratic reorganization. Since 9/11, we seem to be caught in a perpetual loop of reorganizing our homeland security authorities and our intelligence community. The possibility that we need something other than a sweeping organizational fix seldom gets taken seriously. Lawmakers feel any other response would be incommensurate with the original cataclysm, and if they chose such an avenue, they would be showing a lack of seriousness. But while the legislation mandating a great conglomeration of agencies has been enacted, the leadership, vision, and resources to make that "rationalization" effective have been missing. Particularly in the realm of homeland security, the last three years have witnessed an extraordinary amount of wheel-spinning. These were years we could not afford to lose.

More disturbing, the signs are growing that the jihadist threat is a diminishing concern for the nation. Despite clear evidence of an increase of jihadist activity abroad, a recent decline in threat reporting against domestic U.S. targets has led Terrance W. Gainer, the chief of the Capitol Police, to remark in May 2005, "The imminence of a threat seems to have diminished. We're just not as worried as we were a year ago, but we certainly are as vigilant." This from a man whose officers guard a known al Qaeda target, and who is regularly briefed by the FBI [Federal Bureau of Investigation] and CIA [Central Intelligence Agency]. John O. Brennan, then acting director of the new National Counterterrorism Center, agreed, saying, "Progress has been made." The declining sense of urgency has been apparent in President George W. Bush's rhetoric, too. As one observer has noted, Bush mentioned the war on terror or some variant of the phrase more often in the thirty days prior to the 2004 [presidential] election (seventy-one times) than in the six months after (sixty-six times). Before the London attacks in July 2005, only 12 percent of Americans thought of terrorism as the nation's top priority, behind the economy, Iraq, health care, and Social Security—almost a 40 percent drop from the time of the November 2004 election. If past experience holds, this most recent moment of horror will be another brief peak in a downward-moving average.

An argument is now heard that the destruction of the World Trade Center was a once-in-a-millennium lucky shot, that everything broke the hijackers' way. Others observe that the Muslim world has shown itself unwilling to hitch its wagon to bin Laden's mad star, forgetting that acts of jihadist violence are increasing in number and that small opinion changes at the margins of a population of 1.2 billion people can have enormous effects. Although the bad news from Iraq continues to dominate the airwaves, in some ways, Washington in the summer of 2005 feels much as it did in the summer of 1999, when talk of the challenge from China was a dominant theme. Then the question was whether China had stolen satellite technology and interfered in American elections. Now it is China's regional ambitions, its undervalued currency, and its military buildup. Though he has not spoken much of the global terrorist threat of late, [then-]Secretary of Defense Donald Rumsfeld wondered in a major address in June [2005], "Since no nation threatens China, one must wonder: Why this growing investment? Why these continuing large and expanding arms purchases?"

The focus has shifted. Few people are better bellwethers of the zeitgeist [spirit of the times] than *New York Times* columnist Thomas Friedman. His latest book, *The World Is Flat*, a paean to globalization, shot to the top of the bestseller lists when it appeared in April 2005. But for Friedman the globalization that counts is the outsourcing of information technology jobs to Bangalore, manufacturing to China, and the computerization of the Third World—"Everyone in Mali uses

Linux," he exclaims. While Friedman recognizes ... the threat that al Qaeda poses to the benefits of globalization, he makes no acknowledgment of the parallel globalization going on, in which the Internet has accelerated the spread of everything from radical Islamist ideology to the minutiae of bomb making for a growing community of jihadists around the world. The wired world is bringing lightning change to the global security landscape, but all eyes are on how technology is again revolutionizing the marketplace.

At a time when we should be well into our planning for a long conflict, our attention is drifting from the greatest threat we face. It is a recurrent theme in radical Islamist writings that we in the West have a short attention span while the holy warriors of jihad will carry on their fight for as long as they have breath. They look forward, they say over and again, to the day when America returns to its slumbers. If we are indeed doing that, then the true lessons of 9/11 will not be learned until after the next attack.

> *"Terrorism's threat, while real, has been much overblown, something that aids terrorist aims."*

The Threat of Terrorism Is Exaggerated

John Mueller

In the following viewpoint, taken from the introduction to Overblown: How Politicians and the Terrorism Industry Inflate National Security Threats, and Why We Believe Them, *John Mueller argues that the threat of terrorism is exaggerated. Although the odds of dying in a terrorist attack are very small, the author contends, Americans have developed a false sense of insecurity, fostered by the homeland security industry that profits from public funds spent on the war against terrorism. The resulting fear, alarmism, and overreaction, he says, helps the terrorists, damaging the American psyche and economy in ways terrorist acts cannot. Mueller is a professor of political science at Ohio State University where he holds the Woody Hayes Chair of National Security Studies.*

As you read, consider the following questions:

1. According to figures cited by Mueller, what is the life-time probability that someone in the world will die at the hands of terrorists?

2. What noted terrorist does the author quote in support of his argument that fear and overreaction play into the hands of the terrorists?

3. According to the author, what is the likelihood that another attack like the one on 9/11 can take place?

Upon discovering that Weeki Wachee Springs, his Florida roadside water park, had been included on the Department of Homeland Security's list of over 80,000 potential terrorist targets, its marketing and promotion manager, John Athanason, turned reflective. "I can't imagine bin Laden trying to blow up the mermaids," he mused, "but with terrorists, who knows what they're thinking. I don't want to think like a terrorist, but what if the terrorists try to poison the water at Weeki Wachee Springs?"

Whatever his imaginings, however, he went on to report that his enterprise had quickly and creatively risen to the occasion—or seized the opportunity. They were working to get a chunk of the counterterrorism funds allocated to the region by the well-endowed, anxiety-provoking, ever-watchful Department of Homeland Security.

Which is the greater threat: terrorism, or our reaction against it? The Weeki Wachee experience illustrates the problem. A threat that is real but likely to prove to be of limited scope has been massively, perhaps even fancifully, inflated to produce widespread and unjustified anxiety. This process has then led to wasteful, even self-parodic expenditures and policy overreactions, ones that not only very often do more harm and cost more money than anything the terrorists have accomplished, but play into their hands.

The way terrorism anxiety has come to envelop the nation is also illustrated by a casual exchange on television's *60 Minutes*. In an interview, filmmaker-provocateur Michael Moore happened to remark, "The chances of any of us dying in a terrorist incident is very, very, very small," and his interviewer, Bob Simon, promptly admonished, "But no one sees the world like that." Remarkably, both statements are true—the first only a bit more so than the second. It is the thesis of this book that our reaction against terrorism has caused more harm than the threat warrants—not just to civil liberties, not just to the economy, but even to human lives. And our reaction has often helped the terrorists more than it has hurt them. It is the reactive consequences stemming from Simon's perspective—or from what journalist Mark Bowden has characterized as "housewives in Iowa ... watching TV afraid that al-Qaeda's going to charge in their front door"—that generate one of the chief problems presented by terrorism.

International terrorism generally kills a few hundred people a year worldwide—not much more, usually, than the number who drown yearly in bathtubs in the United States. Americans worry intensely about "another 9/11," but if one of these were to occur every three months for the next five years, the chance of being killed in one of them is 0.02 percent. Astronomer Alan Harris has calculated that at present rates, the lifetime probability that a resident of the globe will die at the hands of international terrorists is 1 in 80,000, about the same likelihood that one would die over the same interval from the impact on the earth of an especially ill-directed asteroid or comet.

But such numbers are almost never discussed: Moore's outburst is exceedingly rare. Instead, most Americans seem to have developed a false sense of insecurity about terrorism.

Thus, since 9/11, over a period in which there have been no international terror attacks whatever in the United States and in which an individual's chances of being killed by a terrorist have remained microscopic even if one—or many—did occur, nearly half of the population has continually expressed worry that they or a member of their family will become a victim of terrorism, as the figure shows. Moreover, when asked if they consider another terrorrist attack likely in the United States within the next several months, fewer than 10 percent of Americans usually respond with what has proven to be the correct answer: "Not at all likely." Yet, this group has not notably increased in size despite continual confirmation of its prescience.

That the costs of terrorism chiefly arise from fear and from over-wrought responses holds even for the tragic events of September 11, 2001, which constituted by far the most destructive set of terrorist acts in history and resulted in the deaths of nearly 3,000 people. The economic costs of reaction have been much higher than those inflicted by the terrorists even in that record-shattering episode, and considerably more than 3,000 Americans have died since 9/11 because, out of fear, they drove in cars rather than flew in airplanes, or because they were swept into wars made politically possible by the terrorist events.

Moreover, as terrorist kingpin and devil du jour Osama bin Laden has gleefully noted, fear, alarmism, and overreaction suit the terrorists' agenda just fine because they create the damaging consequences the terrorists seek but are unable to perpetrate on their own. As he put it mockingly in a videotaped message in 2004, it is "easy for us to provoke and bait. . . . All that we have to do is to send two mujahidin . . . to raise a piece of cloth on which is written al-Qaeda in order to make the generals race there to cause America to suffer human, economic, and political losses." His policy, he extravagantly believes, is one of "bleeding America to the point of

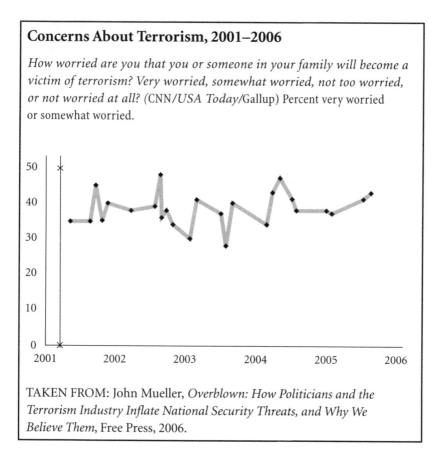

Concerns About Terrorism, 2001–2006

How worried are you that you or someone in your family will become a victim of terrorism? Very worried, somewhat worried, not too worried, or not worried at all? (CNN/USA *Today*/Gallup) Percent very worried or somewhat worried.

TAKEN FROM: John Mueller, *Overblown: How Politicians and the Terrorism Industry Inflate National Security Threats, and Why We Believe Them*, Free Press, 2006.

bankruptcy," and it is one that depends on overreaction by the target: he triumphally points to the fact that the 9/11 terrorist attacks cost al-Qaeda $500,000, while the attack and its aftermath inflicted, he claims, a cost of more than $500 billion on the United States. Shortly after 9/11, he crowed, "America is full of fear from its north to its south, from its west to its east. Thank God for that."

An Unconventional Conventional Wisdom

In exploring these issues, this book develops three themes, in this order: (1) terrorism's threat, while real, has been much overblown, something that aids terrorist aims; (2) this process is a familiar one since, with the benefit of hindsight, we can see that many international threats have been considerably inflated in the past; and (3) applying these lessons, policy toward terrorism should very substantially focus on reducing the damaging fears and overreactions terrorism so routinely fosters.

In the process, I present a considerable number of propositions that, it seems to me, should be—but decidedly aren't—the conventional wisdom on this subject. These propositions are certainly susceptible to debate and to reasoned criticism, but it seems to me that they, rather than their hysterical if attention-grabbing opposites, ought to be the base from which the discussion proceeds. At the very least, they should be part of the policy discussion mix, but they seem almost entirely to have been ignored.

Among these propositions are the following:

- In general, terrorism, particularly international terrorism, doesn't do much damage when considered in almost any reasonable context.

- Although airplanes can still be blown up, another attack like the one on 9/11 is virtually impossible. In 2001 the hijackers had the element of surprise working for them: previous hijackings (including one conducted by Muslim terrorists six months earlier) had mostly been fairly harmless as the perpetrators generally landed the planes somewhere and released, or were forced to release, the passengers. After the 9/11 experience, passengers and crew will fight to prevent a takeover, as was shown on the fourth plane on 9/11.

- The likelihood that any individual American will be killed in a terrorist event is microscopic.

- Just about any damage terrorists are likely to be able to perpetrate can be readily absorbed. To deem the threat an "existential" one is somewhere between extravagant and absurd.

- The capacity of al-Qaeda or of any similar group to do damage in the United States pales in comparison to the capacity other dedicated enemies, particularly international communism, have possessed in the past.

- Lashing out at the terrorist threat is frequently an exercise in self-flagellation because it is usually more expensive than the terrorist attack itself and because it gives the terrorists exactly what they are looking for.

- Chemical and radiological weapons, and most biological ones as well, are incapable of perpetrating mass destruction.

- The likelihood that a terrorist group will be able to master nuclear weapons any time soon is extremely, perhaps vanishingly, small.

- Although murderous and dedicated, al-Qaeda is a very small and very extreme group, and it is unlikely by itself to have the capacity for taking over any significant government.

- Al-Qaeda's terrorist efforts on 9/11 and in the years since have been substantially counterproductive.

- Although additional terrorist attacks in the United States certainly remain possible, an entirely plausible explanation for the fact that there have been none since 2001 is that there is no significant international terrorist presence within the country.

- Policies that continually, or even occasionally, focus entirely on worst-case scenarios (or worst-case fantasies) are unwise and can be exceedingly wasteful.

- In fact, much, probably most of the money and effort expended on counterterrorism since 2001 (and before, for that matter) has been wasted.

- Seeking to protect all potential targets against terrorist attack is impossible and foolish. In fact, just about anything is a potential target.

- Terrorism should be treated essentially as a criminal problem calling mainly for the application of policing methods, particularly in the international sphere, not military ones.

- Because terrorism probably presents only a rather limited threat, a viable policy approach might center around creating the potential to absorb its direct effects and to mitigate its longer range consequences while continuing to support international policing efforts, particularly overseas.

The Role of the Terrorism Industry

One reason these propositions have gone almost entirely unconsidered is that the fears and anxieties created by the 9/11 experience have been so deftly orchestrated and overblown by members of the terrorism industry: politicians, experts, the media, academics, the bureaucracy, and risk entrepreneurs who profit in one way or another by inflating the threat international terrorism is likely to present. For example, in 2003, while Homeland Security czar Tom Ridge was bravely declaring that "America is a country that will not be bent by terror" or "broken by fear," General Richard Myers, chairman of the Joint Chiefs of Staff, was ominously suggesting that if terrorists were able to engineer an event that managed to kill 10,000 Americans, they would successfully "do away with our way of life."

The sudden deaths of that many Americans—although representing fewer than 0.004 percent of the population—would indeed be horrifying and tragic, the greatest one-day disaster the country has suffered since the Civil War. But the United States is hardly likely to be toppled by dramatic acts of terrorist destruction, even extreme ones. The country can readily absorb considerable damage if necessary, and it has outlasted far more potent threats in the past. To suggest otherwise is to express contempt for America's capacity to deal with adversity.

The only way terrorist acts could conceivably "do away with our way of life" would be if, bent and broken, we did it to ourselves in reaction. As broadcaster Edward R. Murrow put it in a different context, "No one can terrorize a whole nation, unless we are all his accomplices." The process would presumably involve repealing the Bill of Rights, boarding up churches, closing down newspapers and media outlets, burning books, abandoning English for North Korean, and refusing evermore to consume hamburgers.

As it is now, terrorism policy constantly seeks to enhance this (rather unlikely) possibility by stoking fear and by engaging in costly, terrorist-encouraging overreaction. For example, the hastily assembled and massively funded Department of Homeland Security officially intones on the first page of its defining manifesto, "Today's terrorists can strike at any place, at any time, and with virtually any weapon." This warning may be true in some sense, of course (depending on how "virtually" is defined), but it is also fatuous and misleading. "Telling Kansan truck drivers to prepare for nuclear terrorism is like telling bullfighters to watch out for lightning. It should not be their primary concern," aptly notes analyst Benjamin Friedman. "For questionable gains in preparedness, we spread paranoia" and facilitate the bureaucratically and politically appealing notion that "if the threat is everywhere, you must spend everywhere," while developing and perpetrating the myth, or at least the impression, that the terrorists are omnipotent and omnipresent.

The department has also urged people to stock up on duct tape and plastic sheeting so they can (almost certainly inadequately) seal off their homes in the wildly unlikely event that a significant chemical or biological attack happened to transpire in their neighborhood. Meanwhile, although it has yet to uncover a single true terrorist cell in the United States, the FBI has warned the citizenry, apparently seriously, to be wary of people bearing almanacs—which, they helpfully explain, contain information of great value to your average diabolical terrorist, such as the location of bridges.

An Alternative Approach to Terrorism

By contrast, a sensible approach to terrorism would support international policing while seeking to reduce terrorism's principal costs—fear, anxiety, and overreaction—not to aggravate them. In the process it would stress that some degree of risk is an inevitable fact of life, that the country can, however grimly, absorb just about any damage terrorism can inflict (it now "absorbs" 40,000 traffic deaths per year, almost all of which could be prevented by imposing a thirteen-mile-per-hour speed limit), and that seeking to protect every imaginable terrorist target (such as Weeki Wachee Springs) is impossible and absurd.

Moreover, there are important economic benefits to such a policy. Effectively it can encourage people to get on airplanes and spend money while their terrified counterparts cower at home, decorate their cars with flag decals, and loudly, defiantly, and pointlessly bellow anthems about "the Home of the Brave." One day we might even begin to consider a heretical possibility, one that may or may not be true but that fits the evidence gathered so far: that the massive Homeland Security apparatus in the United States is persecuting some, spying on many, inconveniencing most, and taxing all to defend against an internal enemy that scarcely exists.

In my view, then, the focus should be on treating terrorism as a criminal activity of rather limited importance and on reducing anxieties and avoiding policy overreaction. These tasks, however, may be exceedingly difficult because fears, once embraced, are not all that susceptible to rational analysis and because the terrorism industry will likely continue assiduously to cultivate those fears.

> *"Because of the things the United States and its allies have done right, al-Qaeda's ability to inflict direct damge in Amerca or on Americans has been sharply reduced."*

The United States Is Winning the War on Terrorism

James Fallows

In the following viewpoint, James Fallows argues that America is winning the war on terrorism. Dispersal of the Taliban and destruction of training camps in Afghanistan has crippled al Qaeda, he contends. Electronic surveillance now prevents al Qaeda leaders from using satellite phones and cell phones to communicate, Fallows adds, and new terrorist groups are dispersed and lack the ability to coordinate a large-scale attack, making another 9/11 unlikely. Fallows is a national correspondent for the Atlantic Monthly.

As you read, consider the following questions:

1. According to Fallows, how has the ability of al Qaeda to transfer money been affected by international surveillance systems?

2. In the view of the military historian quoted by Fallows, how important to terrorist activity is Osama bin Laden?

3. According to experts quoted by the author, what change in domestic policies has had the biggest protective effect on security against terrorist acts in America?

Osama bin Laden's public statements are those of a fanatic. But they often reveal a canny ability to size up the strengths and weaknesses of both allies and enemies, especially the United States. In his videotaped statement just days before the 2004 U.S. presidential election, bin Laden mocked the [George W.] Bush administration for being unable to find him, for letting itself become mired in Iraq, and for refusing to come to grips with al-Qaeda's basic reason for being. One example: "Contrary to Bush's claim that we hate freedom, let him explain to us why we don't strike, for example, Sweden?" Bin Laden also boasted about how easy it had become for him "to provoke and bait" the American leadership: "All that we have to do is to send two mujahideen . . . to raise a piece of cloth on which is written 'al-Qaeda' in order to make the generals race there."

Perhaps al-Qaeda's leaders, like most people, cannot turn a similarly cold eye upon themselves. A purely realistic self-assessment must be all the more difficult for leaders who say that their struggle may last for centuries and that their guidance comes from outside this world. But what if al-Qaeda's leaders could see their faults and weaknesses as clearly as they see those of others? What if they had a Clausewitz or a Sun Tzu [Carl von Clausewitz and Sun Tzu were famous military strategists] to speak frankly to them?

This spring and summer [2006], I talked with some sixty experts about the current state of the conflict that bin Laden thinks of as the "world jihad"—and that the U.S. government has called both the "global war on terror" and the "long war." I wanted to know how it looked from the terrorists' perspective. What had gone better than expected? What had gone worse? Could bin Laden assume, on any grounds other than pure faith, that the winds of history were at his back? Could he and his imitators count on a growing advantage because technology has made it so easy for individuals to inflict mass damage, and because politics and the media have made it so hard for great powers to fight dirty, drawn-out wars? Or might his strategists have to conclude that, at least for this stage of what they envision as a centuries-long struggle, their best days had passed?

Al Qaeda Is Losing

About half of the authorities I spoke with were from military or intelligence organizations; the others were academics or members of think tanks, plus a few businesspeople. Half were Americans; the rest were Europeans, Middle Easterners, Australians, and others. [In 2002], most of these people had supported the decision to invade Iraq. Although they now said that the war had been a mistake (followed by what nearly all viewed as a disastrously mismanaged occupation), relatively few said that the United States should withdraw anytime soon. The reasons most of them gave were the need for America to make good on commitments, the importance of keeping the Sunni parts of Iraq from turning into a new haven for global terrorists, and the chance that conditions in Iraq would eventually improve.

The initial surprise for me was how little fundamental disagreement I heard about how the situation looks through bin Laden's eyes. While the people I spoke with differed on details, and while no one put things exactly the way I am about to here, there was consensus on the main points.

The larger and more important surprise was the implicit optimism about the U.S. situation that came through in these accounts—not on Iraq but on the fight against al-Qaeda and the numerous imitators it has spawned. For the past five years the United States has assumed itself to be locked in "asymmetric warfare," with the advantages on the other side. Any of the tens of millions of foreigners entering the country each year could, in theory, be an enemy operative—to say nothing of the millions of potential recruits already here. Any of the dozens of ports, the scores of natural-gas plants and nuclear facilities, the hundreds of important bridges and tunnels, or the thousands of shopping malls, office towers, or sporting facilities could be the next target of attack. It is impossible to protect them all, and even trying could ruin America's social fabric and public finances. The worst part of the situation is helplessness, as America's officials and its public wait for an attack they know they cannot prevent.

Viewing the world from al-Qaeda's perspective, though, reveals the underappreciated advantage on America's side. The struggle does remain asymmetric, but it may have evolved in a way that gives target countries, especially the United States, more leverage and control than we have assumed. Yes, there could be another attack tomorrow, and most authorities assume that some attempts to blow up trains, bridges, buildings, or airplanes in America will eventually succeed. No modern nation is immune to politically inspired violence, and even the best-executed antiterrorism strategy will not be airtight.

But the overall prospect looks better than many Americans believe, and better than nearly all political rhetoric asserts. The essence of the change is this: because of al-Qaeda's own mistakes, and because of the things the United States and its allies have done right, al-Qaeda's ability to inflict direct damage in America or on Americans has been sharply reduced. Its successor groups in Europe, the Middle East, and elsewhere will continue to pose dangers. But its hopes for fundamentally harming the United States now rest less on what it can do itself than on what it can trick, tempt, or goad us into doing. Its destiny is no longer in its own hands.

Overreaction Is the Danger

"Does al-Qaeda still constitute an 'existential' threat?" asks David Kilcullen, who has written several influential papers on the need for a new strategy against Islamic insurgents. Kilcullen, who as an Australian army officer commanded counterinsurgency units in East Timor, recently served as an adviser in the Pentagon and is now a senior adviser on counterterrorism at the State Department. He was referring to the argument about whether the terrorism of the twenty-first century endangers the very existence of the United States and its allies, as the Soviet Union's nuclear weapons did throughout the Cold War (and as the remnants of that arsenal still might).

"I think it does, but not for the obvious reasons," Kilcullen told me. He said the most useful analogy was the menace posed by European anarchists in the nineteenth century. "If you add up everyone they personally killed, it came to maybe 2,000 people, which is not an existential threat." But one of their number assassinated Archduke Franz Ferdinand and his wife. The act itself took the lives of two people. The unthinking response of European governments in effect started World War I. "So because of the reaction they provoked, they were able to kill millions of people and destroy a civilization.

"It is not the people al-Qaeda might kill that is the threat," he concluded. "*Our reaction* is what can cause the damage. It's al-Qaeda plus our response that creates the existential danger."

Since 9/11, this equation has worked in al-Qaeda's favor. That can be reversed.

What Has Gone Wrong for Al Qaeda

Brian Michael Jenkins, a veteran terrorism expert at the RAND Corporation, recently published a book called *Unconquerable Nation: Knowing Our Enemy, Strengthening Ourselves*. It includes a fictional briefing, in Osama bin Laden's mountain stronghold, by an al-Qaeda strategist assigned to sum up the state of world jihad five years after the 9/11 attacks. "Any al-

Qaeda briefer would have to acknowledge that the past five years have been difficult," Jenkins says. His fictional briefer summarizes for bin Laden what happened after 9/11: "The Taliban were dispersed, and al-Qaeda's training camps in Afghanistan were dismantled." Al-Qaeda operatives by the thousands have been arrested, detained, or killed. So have many members of the crucial al-Qaeda leadership circle around bin Laden and his chief strategist, Ayman al-Zawahiri. Moreover, Jenkins's briefer warns, it has become harder for the remaining al-Qaeda leaders to carry out the organization's most basic functions: "Because of increased intelligence efforts by the United States and its allies, transactions of any type—communications, travel, money transfers—have become more dangerous for the jihadists. Training and operations have been decentralized, raising the risk of fragmentation and loss of unity. Jihadists everywhere face the threat of capture or martyrdom."

Michael Scheuer was chief of the CIA's Osama bin Laden unit from 1995 to 1999 and was a special adviser to it for three years after 9/11 (the CIA disbanded the unit [in the summer of 2006]). In a similar mock situation report that Scheuer has presented at military conferences, a fictional briefer tells his superiors in al-Qaeda: "We must always keep in focus the huge downside of this war. We are, put simply, being hunted and attacked by the most powerful nation in the history of the world. And despite the heavy personnel losses we have suffered, may God accept them as martyrs, the United States has not yet made the full destructiveness of its power felt."

Al-Qaeda Central Is Gone

Any assessment of the world five years after 9/11 begins with the damage inflicted on "Al-Qaeda Central"—the organization led by bin Laden and al-Zawahiri that, from the late 1990s onward, both inspired and organized the worldwide anti-American campaign. "Their command structure is gone, their

Killing Muslims Has Damaged Al Qaida's Credibility

Al-Qaida's support in the Muslim world has plummeted, partly because of the terror group's lack of success in Iraq, more because al-Qaida's attacks have mostly killed Muslim civilians.

"Iraq has proved to be the graveyard, not just of many al-Qaida operatives, but of the organization's reputation as a defender of Islam," said StrategyPage.com.

Jack Kelly, Pittsburgh Post-Gazette, *November 17, 2007.*

Afghan sanctuary is gone, their ability to move around and hold meetings is gone, their financial and communications networks have been hit hard," says Seth Stodder, a former official in the Department of Homeland Security (DHS).

Kilcullen says, "The al-Qaeda that existed in 2001 simply no longer exists. In 2001 it was a relatively centralized organization, with a planning hub, a propaganda hub, a leadership team, all within a narrow geographic area. All that is gone, because we destroyed it." Where bin Laden's central leadership team could once wire money around the world using normal bank networks, it now must rely on couriers with vests full of cash. (I heard this point frequently in interviews, weeks before the controversial news stories revealing that the U.S. government had in fact been tracking international bank transfers. Everyone I spoke with assumed that some sort of tracking was firmly in place—and that the commanders of al-Qaeda had changed their behavior in a way that showed they were aware of it as well.) Where bin Laden's network could once use satellite phones and the Internet for communication, it now has to avoid most forms of electronic communication, which leave an electronic trail back to the user. Bin Laden and al-Zawahiri now send information out through videotapes and via operatives in Internet chat rooms. "The Internet is all well and good, but it's not like meeting face to face or conducting training," says Peter Bergen, author of *The Osama bin Laden I Know*. "Their reliance on it is a sign of their weakness."

Scheuer, Richard Clarke (the former White House terrorism adviser), and others have long complained that following the bombing of the U.S.S. *Cole*, in 2000, the United States should have been prepared to launch a retaliatory raid on Afghanistan immediately after any successor attack—"the next day!" Scheuer told me—rather than taking several weeks to strike, and that it might well have chased down and eliminated bin Laden and al-Zawahiri if it had concentrated on them throughout 2002 rather than being distracted into Iraq. Nonetheless, most experts agree that the combination of routing the Taliban, taking away training camps, policing the financial networks, killing many al-Qaeda lieutenants, and maintaining electronic and aerial surveillance has put bin Laden and al-Zawahiri in a situation in which they can survive and inspire but not do much more.

Bin Laden Now Irrelevant

"Al-Qaeda has taken some very hard blows," Martin van Creveld, a military historian at the Hebrew University of Jerusalem and the author of *The Transformation of War* and other books, told me. "Osama bin Laden is almost irrelevant, from an operational point of view. This is one reason why he has to keep releasing videos."

Does this matter, given bin Laden's elevation to Che Guevara-like symbolic status [Guevara was a Marxist revolutionary during the 1950s and 1960s who played a pivotal role in the Cuban Revolution and who gained folkhero status after his death in 1967] and his ability to sneak out no fewer than twenty-four recorded messages between 9/11 and the summer of [2006]? "For bin Laden, it's clearly a consolation prize to become a 'philosophy' rather than an organization," says Caleb Carr, a history professor at Bard College and the author of *The Lessons of Terror*. "They already were a global philosophy, but they used to have a command structure too. It's like the difference between Marxism and Leninism, and they're back to just being Marx." Marc Sageman, author of *Understanding Terror Networks*, says that before 9/11, people attracted to the terrorist cause could come to Afghanistan for camaraderie, indoctrination, and specific operational training. "Now you can't *find* al-Qaeda, so it's difficult to join them," he told me. "People have to figure out what to do on their own."

The shift from a coherent Al-Qaeda Central to a global proliferation of "self-starter" terrorist groups—those inspired by bin Laden's movement but not coordinated by it—has obviously not eliminated the danger of attacks. In different ways, the bombings in Madrid in 2004, in Bali and London in 2005, and in Iraq throughout the [war there] all illustrate the menace—and, in the view of many people I spoke with, prefigure the threats—that could arise in the United States. But the shift to these successor groups has made it significantly harder for terrorists of any provenance to achieve what all of them would like: a "second 9/11," a large-scale attack on the U.S. mainland that would kill hundreds or thousands of people and terrorize hundreds of millions.

Another Big Attack Unlikely

I asked everyone I spoke with some variant of the familiar American question: Why, through nearly five years after 9/11, had there not been another big attack on U.S. soil? People prefaced their replies with reminders that the future is unknowable, that the situation could change tomorrow, and that the reasons for America's safety so far were not fully understood. But most then went on to say that another shocking,

9/11-scale coordinated attack was probably too hard for today's atomized terrorist groups to pull off.

The whole array of "homeland security" steps had made the United States a somewhat more difficult target to attack, most people said. But not a single person began the list of important post-9/11 changes with these real, if modest, measures of domestic protection. Indeed, nearly all emphasized the haphazard, wasteful, and sometimes self-defeating nature of the DHS's approach.

"It is harder to get into the country—to a fault," says Seth Stodder. Much tougher visa rules, especially for foreign students, have probably kept future Mohammed Attas out of flight schools. But they may also be keeping out future Andrew Groves and Sergey Brins. (Grove, born in Hungary, cofounded Intel; Brin, born in Russia, cofounded Google.) "The student-visa crackdown was to deal with Atta," Stodder says. "It's affecting the commanding heights of our tech economy." Richard Clarke says that the domestic change that has had the biggest protective effect is not any governmental measure but an increased public scrutiny of anyone who "looks Muslim." "It's a terrible, racist reaction," Clarke says, "but it has made it harder for them to operate."

The DHS now spends $42 billion a year on its vast range of activities, which include FEMA [Federal Emergency Management Agency] and other disaster-relief efforts, the Coast Guard, immigration, and border and customs operations. Of this, about $5 billion goes toward screening passengers at airports. The widely held view among security experts is that this airport spending is largely for show. Strengthened cockpit doors and a flying public that knows what happened on 9/11 mean that commercial airliners are highly unlikely to be used again as targeted flying bombs. "The inspection process is mostly security theater, to make people feel safe about flying," says John Mueller, a political scientist at Ohio State and the author of a forthcoming book about the security-industrial complex. He adds that because fears "are not purely rational, if it makes people feel better, the effort may be worth it."

Nothing Will Top 9/11

John Robb, a former clandestine-operations specialist for the Air Force who now writes a blog called "Global Guerrillas," says that it is relatively easy for terrorists to disrupt society's normal operations—think of daily life in Israel, or England under assault from the IRA [Irish Republican Army]. But large-scale symbolic shock, of the type so stunningly achieved on 9/11 and advocated by bin Laden ever since, is difficult to repeat or sustain. "There are diminishing returns on symbolic terrorism," Robb told me. "Each time it happens, the public becomes desensitized, and the media pays less attention." To maintain the level of terror, each attack must top the previous one—and in Robb's view, "nothing will ever top 9/11." He allows for the obvious and significant exception of terrorists getting hold of a nuclear weapon. But, like most people I interviewed, he says this is harder and less likely than the public assumes. Moreover, if nuclear weapons constitute the one true existential threat, then countering the proliferation of those weapons themselves is what American policy should address, more than fighting terrorism in general. For a big, coordinated, nonnuclear attack, he says, "the number of people involved is substantial, the lead time is long, the degree of coordination is great, and the specific skills you need are considerable. It's not realistic for al-Qaeda anymore."

American Muslims Immune to Jihadism

Bruce Hoffman, a terrorism expert at Georgetown University and the author of *Inside Terrorism* and other books, says that the 9/11-style spectacular attack remains fundamental to Osama bin Laden's hopes, because of his belief that it would "catapult him back into being in charge of the movement." Robb's fear is that after being thwarted in their quest to blow

up the Rose Bowl or the Capitol, today's loosely affiliated terrorists will turn to the smaller-scale attacks on economic targets—power plants, rail lines—that are very hard to prevent
and can do tremendous cumulative damage.

The dispersed nature of the new al-Qaeda creates other
difficulties for potential terrorists. For one, the recruitment of
self-starter cells within the United States is thought to have
failed so far. Spain, England, France, and the Netherlands are
among the countries alarmed to find Islamic extremists among
people whose families have lived in Europe for two or three
generations. "The patriotism of the American Muslim community has been grossly underreported," says Marc Sageman,
who has studied the process by which people decide to join or
leave terrorist networks. According to Daniel Benjamin, a
former official on the National Security Council and coauthor
of *The Next Attack*, Muslims in America "have been our first
line of defense." Even though many have been "unnerved by a
law-enforcement approach that might have been inevitable
but was still disturbing," the community has been "pretty
much immune to the jihadist virus."

"The preventive paradigm has compromised our spirit, strengthened our enemies and left us less free and less safe."

The United States Is Losing the War on Terrorism

David Cole and Jules Lobel

In the following viewpoint, David Cole and Jules Lobel argue that the "preventive paradigm" method of fighting terrorism in the United States has failed. This approach, say the authors, discriminates against Arabs and Muslims, violates the rights of innocent citizens, and has resulted in few convictions of terrorists. Cole and Lobel also assert that the war in Iraq has diverted resources from fighting al Qaeda. According to foreign policy experts cited by the authors, the United States is not winning the war on terror. David Cole is a legal affairs correspondent for the Nation *and a professor at Georgetown University Law Center. Jules Lobel is a professor of law at the University of Pittsburgh. They are coauthors of the book* Less Safe, Less Free: Why America Is Losing the War on Terror.

As you read, consider the following questions:

1. How many "national security letters" have been served on businesses by the FBI, according to the authors?

David Cole and Jules Lobel, "Why We're Losing the War on Terror," *The Nation*, September 24, 2007. www.thenation.com. Reproduced by permission.

2. How many al Qaeda sleeper cells in the United States have been uncovered by the FBI, according to Cole and Lobel?

3. How does the government's success rate in cases alleging terrorist activities since 9/11 compare with their conviction rate for felonies overall, according to the authors?

President George W. Bush is fond of reminding us that no terrorist attacks have occurred on domestic soil since 9/11. But has the Administration's "war on terror" actually made us safer? According to the July 2007 National Intelligence Estimate, Al Qaeda has fully reconstituted itself in Pakistan's northern border region. Terrorist attacks worldwide have grown dramatically in frequency and lethality since 2001. New terrorist groups, from Al Qaeda in Mesopotamia to the small groups of young men who bombed subways and buses in London [July 2005] and Madrid [March 2004] have multiplied since 9/11. Meanwhile, despite the Bush Administration's boasts, the total number of people it has convicted of engaging in a terrorist act since 9/11 is one (Richard Reid, the shoe bomber).

Nonetheless, leading [2008] Democratic presidential candidate Hillary Clinton claims that we are safer. Republican candidate Rudy Giuliani warns that "the next election is about whether we go back on defense against terrorism . . . or are we going to go on offense." And Democrats largely respond by insisting that they, too, would "go on offense." Few have asked whether "going on offense" actually works as a counterterrorism strategy. It doesn't. The Bush strategy has been a colossal failure, not only in terms of constitutional principle but in terms of national security. It turns out that in fighting terrorism, the best defense is not a good offense but a smarter defense.

Preventive Paradigm Violates Rights

"Going on offense," or the "paradigm of prevention," as then-Attorney General John Ashcroft dubbed it, has touched all of us. Some, like Canadian Maher Arar, have been rendered to third countries (in his case, Syria) to be interrogated by security services known for torture. Others have been subjected to months of virtually nonstop questioning, sexual abuse, waterboarding and injections with intravenous fluids until they urinate on themselves. Still others, like KindHearts, an American charity in Toledo, Ohio, have had their assets frozen under the USA Patriot Act and all their records seized without so much as a charge, much less a finding, of wrongdoing.

In the name of the "preventive paradigm," thousands of Arab and Muslim immigrants have been singled out, essentially on the basis of their ethnicity or religion, for special treatment, including mandatory registration, FBI interviews and preventive detention. Businesses have been served with more than 100,000 "national security letters," which permit the FBI to demand records on customers without a court order or individualized basis for suspicion. We have all been subjected to unprecedented secrecy about what elected officials are doing in our name while simultaneously suffering unprecedented official intrusion into our private lives by increased video surveillance, warrantless wiretapping and datamining. Most tragically, more than 3,700 Americans and more than 70,000 Iraqi civilians have given their lives for the "preventive paradigm," which was used to justify going to war against a country that had not attacked us and posed no imminent threat of attack.

The preventive paradigm had its genesis on September 12, 2001. In *Bush at War*, Bob Woodward recounts a White House meeting in which FBI Director Robert Mueller advised that authorities must take care not to taint evidence in seeking 9/11 accomplices so that they could eventually be held accountable. Ashcroft immediately objected, saying, "The chief mission of US law enforcement . . . is to stop another attack and apprehend any accomplices. . . . If we can't bring them to trial, so be it." Ever since, the "war on terror" has been characterized by highly coercive, "forward-looking" pre-emptive measures—warrantless wiretapping, detention, coercive interrogation, even war—undertaken not on evidence of past or current wrongdoing but on speculation about future threats.

Coercion Without Probable Cause

In isolation, neither the goal of preventing future attacks nor the tactic of using coercive measures is novel or troubling. All law enforcement seeks to prevent crime, and coercion is a necessary element of state power. However, when the end of prevention and the means of coercion are combined in the Administration's preventive paradigm, they produce a troubling form of anticipatory state violence—undertaken before wrongdoing has actually occurred and often without good evidence for believing that wrongdoing will ever occur.

The Bush strategy turns the law's traditional approach to state coercion on its head. With narrow exceptions, the rule of law reserves invasions of privacy, detention, punishment and use of military force for those who have been shown—on the basis of sound evidence and fair procedures—to have committed or to be plotting some wrong. The police can tap phones or search homes, but only when there is probable cause to believe that a crime has been committed and that the search is likely to find evidence of the crime. People can be preventively detained pending trial, but only when there is both probable cause of past wrongdoing and concrete evidence that they pose a danger to the community or are likely to abscond if left at large. And under international law, nations may use military force unilaterally only in response to an objectively verifiable attack or threat of imminent attack.

These bedrock legal requirements are a hindrance to "going on offense." Accordingly, the Administration has asserted sweeping executive discretion, eschewed questions of guilt or innocence and substituted secrecy and speculation for accountability and verifiable fact. Where the rule of law demands fair and open procedures, the preventive paradigm employs truncated processes often conducted in secret, denying the accused a meaningful opportunity to respond. The need for pre-emptive action is said to justify secrecy and shortcuts, whatever the cost to innocents. Where the rule of law demands that people be held liable only for their own actions, the Administration has frequently employed guilt by association and ethnic profiling to target suspected future wrongdoers. And where the rule of law absolutely prohibits torture and disappearances, the preventive paradigm views these tactics as lesser evils to defuse the proverbial ticking time bomb.

All other things being equal, preventing a terrorist act is, of course, preferable to responding after the fact—all the more so when the threats include weapons of mass destruction and our adversaries are difficult to detect, willing to kill themselves and seemingly unconstrained by any recognizable considerations of law, morality or human dignity. But there are plenty of preventive counterterrorism measures that conform to the rule of law, such as increased protections at borders and around vulnerable targets, institutional reforms designed to encourage better information sharing, even military force and military detention when employed in self-defense. The real problems arise when the state uses highly coercive measures—depriving people of their life, liberty or property, or going to war—based on speculation, without adhering to the laws long seen as critical to regulating and legitimizing such force.

Even if one were to accept as a moral or ethical matter the "ends justify the means" rationales advanced for the preventive paradigm, the paradigm fails its own test: There is little or no evidence that the Administration's coercive pre-emptive measures have made us safer, and substantial evidence that they have in fact exacerbated the dangers we face.

Preventive Coercion Does Not Work

Consider the costliest example: the war in Iraq. Precisely because the preventive doctrine turns on speculation about non-imminent events, it permitted the Administration to turn its focus from Al Qaeda, the organization that attacked us on 9/11, to Iraq, a nation that did not. The Iraq War has by virtually all accounts made the United States, the Iraqi people, many of our allies and for that matter much of the world more vulnerable to terrorists. By targeting Iraq, the Bush Administration not only siphoned off much-needed resources from the struggle against Al Qaeda but also created a golden opportunity for Al Qaeda to inspire and recruit others to attack US and allied targets. And our invasion of Iraq has turned it into the world's premier terrorist training ground.

The preventive paradigm has been no more effective in other aspects of the "war on terror." According to US figures, international terrorist attacks increased by 300 percent between 2003 and 2004. In 2005 alone, there were 360 suicide bombings, resulting in 3,000 deaths, compared with an annual average of about ninety such attacks over the five preceding years. That hardly constitutes progress.

But what about the fact that, other than the anthrax mailings in 2001, there has not been another terrorist attack in the United States since 9/11? The real question, of course, is whether the Administration's coercive preventive measures can be credited for that. There were eight years between the first and second attacks on the World Trade Center. And when one looks at what the preventive paradigm has come up with in terms of concrete results, it's an astonishingly thin file. At Guantánamo, for example, once said to house "the worst of the worst," the Pentagon's Combatant Status Review Tribunals' own findings categorized only 8 percent of some 500 detainees held there in 2006 as fighters for Al Qaeda or the Taliban. More than half of the 775 Guantánamo detainees have now been released, suggesting that they may not have been "the worst of the worst" after all.

As for terror cells at home, the FBI admitted in February 2005 that it had yet to identify a single Al Qaeda sleeper cell in the entire United States. And it hasn't found any since— unless you count the Florida group arrested in 2006, whose principal step toward an alleged plot to blow up the Sears Tower was to order combat boots and whose only Al Qaeda "connection" was to a federal informant pretending to be Al Qaeda.

Few Terrorism Convictions

The Justice Department claims on its website to have charged more than 400 people in "terrorism-related" cases, but its own Inspector General has criticized those figures as inflated. The vast majority of the cases involved not terrorism but minor nonviolent offenses such as immigration fraud, credit-card fraud or lying to an FBI agent. The *New York Times* and the *Washington Post* found that only thirty-nine of the convictions were for a terrorism crime. And virtually all of those were for "material support" to groups labeled terrorist, a crime that requires no proof that the defendant ever intended to further a terrorist act. While prosecutors have obtained a handful of convictions for conspiracy to engage in terrorism, several of those convictions rest on extremely broad statutes that don't require proof of any specific plan or act, or on questionable entrapment tactics by government informants.

Many of the Administration's most highly touted "terrorism" cases have disintegrated after the Justice Department's initial self-congratulatory press conference announcing the indictment, most notably those against Capt. James Yee, a Muslim chaplain at Guantánamo initially accused of being a spy; Sami Al-Arian, a computer science professor acquitted on

Al Qaeda Continues to Be a Threat

[Frances Fragos] Townsend [head of the Homeland Security Council in 2007] declined to describe what may be alternative strategies for dealing with the Qaeda threat in Pakistan, but acknowledged frustration that Al Qaeda was succeeding in rebuilding its infrastructure and its links to affiliates, while keeping Mr. bin Laden and his top lieutenants alive for nearly six years since the Sept. 11 attacks.

The July [2007] intelligence report, known as a National Intelligence Estimate, represents the consensus view of all 16 agencies that make up the American intelligence community. The report concluded that the United States would face a "persistent and evolving terrorist threat over the next three years."

Mark Mazzetti and David E. Sanger,
New York Times, July 18, 2007.

charges of conspiracy to kill Americans; Muhammad Salah and Abdelhaleem Ashqar, acquitted in Chicago of aiding Hamas; Sami al-Hussayen, a Saudi student acquitted by an Idaho jury of charges that he had aided terrorism by posting links on his website to other sites containing jihadist rhetoric; and Yaser Hamdi, the US citizen held for years as an enemy combatant but released from military custody when the government faced the prospect of having to prove that he was an enemy combatant. The Administration recently managed to convict José Padilla, the other US citizen held as an enemy combatant, not for any of the terrorist plots against the United States that it once accused him of hatching but for attending an Al Qaeda training camp and conspiring to support Muslim rebels in Chechnya and Bosnia before 9/11.

Overall, the government's success rate in cases alleging terrorist charges since 9/11 is only 29 percent, compared with a 92 percent conviction rate for felonies. This is an astounding statistic, because presumably federal juries are not predisposed to sympathize with Arab or Muslim defendants accused of terrorism. But when one prosecutes prematurely, failure is often the result.

The government's "preventive" immigration initiatives have come up even more empty-handed. After 9/11 the Bush Administration called in 80,000 foreign nationals for fingerprinting, photographing and "special registration" simply because they came from predominantly Arab or Muslim countries; sought out another 8,000 young men from the same countries for FBI interviews; and placed more than 5,000 foreign nationals here in preventive detention. Yet as of September 2007, not one of these people stands convicted of a terrorist crime. The government's record, in what is surely the largest campaign of ethnic profiling since the Japanese internment of World War II, is 0 for 93,000.

Experts Say Terrorists Are Winning

These statistics offer solid evidence to support the overwhelming consensus that *Foreign Policy* found when it polled more than 100 foreign policy experts—evenly dispersed along the political spectrum—and found that 91 percent felt that the world is becoming more dangerous for the United States, and that 84 percent said we are not winning the "war on terror."

It is certainly possible that some of these preventive measures deterred would-be terrorists from attacking us or helped to uncover and foil terrorist plots before they could come to fruition. But if real plots had been foiled and real terrorists identified, one would expect some criminal convictions to follow. When FBI agents successfully foiled a plot by Sheik Omar Abdel Rahman (popularly known as "the blind sheik") and others to bomb bridges and tunnels around Manhattan in the 1990s, it also convicted the plotters and sent them to prison for life.

In October 2005 Bush claimed that the United States and its allies had foiled ten terrorist plots. But he couldn't point to a single convicted terrorist. Consider just one of Bush's ten "success" stories, the one about which he provided the most details: an alleged Al Qaeda plot to fly an airplane into the Library Tower, a skyscraper in Los Angeles. The perpetrators, described only as Southeast Asians, were said to have been captured in early 2002 in Asia. As far as we know, however, no one has ever been charged or tried for this alleged terror plot. Intelligence officials told the *Washington Post* that there was "deep disagreement within the intelligence community about . . . whether it was ever much more than talk." A senior FBI official said, "To take that and make it into a disrupted plot is just ludicrous." American officials claim to have learned about some of the plot's details by interrogating captured Al Qaeda leader Khalid Shaikh Mohammed, but he was captured in 2003, long after the perpetrators had been arrested. As the *Los Angeles Times* put it, "By the time anybody knew about it, the threat—if there had been one—had passed, federal counter-terrorism officials said." These facts—all omitted in Bush's re-telling—suggest that such claims of success need to be viewed skeptically.

Preventive Paradigm Makes Us Less Secure

If the Bush strategy were merely ineffectual, that would be bad enough. But it's worse than that; the President's policy has actually made us significantly less secure. While the Administration has concentrated on swaggeringly aggressive coercive initiatives of dubious effect, it has neglected less dramatic but more effective preventive initiatives. In December 2005 the bipartisan 9/11 Commission gave the Administration failing or near-failing grades on many of the most basic domestic security measures, including assessing critical infrastructure vulnerabilities, securing weapons of mass destruction, screening airline passengers and cargo, sharing information between law enforcement and intelligence agencies, insuring that first responders have adequate communications and supporting secular education in Muslim countries. We spend more in a day in Iraq than we do annually on some of the most important defensive initiatives here at home.

The preventive paradigm has also made it more difficult to bring terrorists to justice, just as FBI Director Mueller warned on September 12. When the Administration chooses to disappear suspects into secret prisons and use waterboarding to encourage them to talk, it forfeits any possibility of bringing the suspects to justice for their alleged crimes, because evidence obtained coercively at a "black site" would never be admissible in a fair and legitimate trial. That's the real reason no one has yet been brought to trial at Guantánamo. There is debate about whether torture ever results in reliable intelligence—but there can be no debate that it radically curtails the government's ability to bring a terrorist to justice.

Paradigm Alienates Potential Allies

Assuming that the principal terrorist threat still comes from Al Qaeda or, more broadly, a violence-prone fundamentalist strain of Islam, and that the "enemies" in this struggle are a relatively small number of Arab and Muslim men, it is all the more critical that we develop close, positive ties with Arab and Muslim communities here and abroad. By alienating those whose help we need most, the preventive paradigm has had exactly the opposite effect.

At the same time, we have given Al Qaeda the best propaganda it could ever have hoped for. Then-Defense Secretary Donald Rumsfeld identified the critical question in an October 2003 internal Pentagon memo: "Are we capturing, killing or deterring and dissuading more terrorists every day than the madrassas and the radical clerics are recruiting, training and deploying against us?" While there is no precise metric for answering Rumsfeld's question, there can be little doubt that our preventive tactics have been a boon to terrorist recruitment throughout the world.

More broadly still, our actions have radically undermined our standing in the world. The damage to US prestige was perhaps most dramatically revealed when, after the report of CIA black sites surfaced in November 2005, Russia, among several other countries, promptly issued a press release claiming that it had nothing to do with the sites. When Russia feels the need to distance itself from the United States out of concern that its human rights image might be tarnished by association, we have fallen far.

In short, we have gone from being the object of the world's sympathy immediately after 9/11 to being the country most likely to be hated. Anti-Americanism is at an all-time high. In some countries, Osama bin Laden has a higher approval rating than the United States. And much of the anti-Americanism is tied to the perception that the United States has pursued its "war on terror" in an arrogant, unilateral fashion, defying the very values we once championed.

Law and Liberty Key to Security

The Bush Administration just doesn't get it. Its National Defense Strategy, published by the Pentagon, warns that "our strength as a nation state will continue to be challenged by those who employ a strategy of the weak using international fora, judicial processes, and terrorism." The proposition that judicial processes and international accountability—the very essence of the rule of law—are to be dismissed as a strategy of the weak, aligned with terrorism itself, makes clear that the

Administration has come to view the rule of law as an obstacle, not an asset, in its effort to protect us from terrorist attack.

Our long-term security turns not on "going on offense" by locking up thousands of "suspected terrorists" who turn out to have no connection to terrorism; nor on forcing suspects to bark like dogs, urinate and defecate on themselves, and endure sexual humiliation; nor on attacking countries that have not threatened to attack us. Security rests not on exceptionalism and double standards but on a commitment to fairness, justice and the rule of law. The rule of law in no way precludes a state from defending itself from terrorists but requires that it do so within constraints. And properly understood, those constraints are assets, not obstacles. Aharon Barak, who recently retired as president of Israel's Supreme Court, said it best in a case forbidding the use of "moderate physical pressure" in interrogating Palestinian terror suspects: "A democracy must sometimes fight terror with one hand tied behind its back. Even so, a democracy has the upper hand. The rule of law and the liberty of an individual constitute important components in its understanding of security. At the end of the day, they strengthen its spirit and this strength allows it to overcome its difficulties."

The preventive paradigm has compromised our spirit, strengthened our enemies and left us less free and less safe. If we are ready to learn from our mistakes, however, there is a better way to defend ourselves—through, rather than despite, a recommitment to the rule of law.

Periodical Bibliography

The following articles have been selected to supplement the diverse views presented in this chapter.

Fouad Ajami   "No Surrender," *Wall Street Journal*, Eastern Edition, March 19, 2008.

Graham Allison   "Is Nuclear Terrorism a Threat to Canada's National Security?" *International Journal*, July 1, 2005.

Margaret Beckett   "Transnational Terrorism: Defeating the Threat," *RUSI Journal*, December 1, 2006.

Economist   "Feel Safer Now?" March 8, 2008.

Nabil Fahmy   "Terrorism Is the World's Problem," *Duke Journal of Comparative & International Law*, vol. 16, no. 157, 2006.

Homeland Security Advisory Council   "Report of the Future of Terrorism Task Force," January 2007. www.dhs.gov/xlibrary/assets/hsac-future-terrorism-010107.pdf.

Nicholas Johnson   "General Semantics, Terrorism and War," *Et Cetera*, January 1, 2007.

William R. Johnstone   "Not Safe Enough: Fixing Transportation Security," *Issues in Science and Technology*, January 1, 2007.

Rafael Llorca-Vivero   "Terrorism and International Tourism: New Evidence," *Defence & Peace Economics*, April 2008.

Peter Marcuse   "The Threat of 'Terrorism' and the Right to the City," *Fordham Urban Law Journal*, July 1, 2005.

Magnus Ranstorp   "Countering Terrorism: Can We Meet the Threat of Global Violence?" *RUSI Journal*, August 1, 2007.

OPPOSING
VIEWPOINTS®
SERIES

CHAPTER 2

How Is Society Susceptible to Terrorism?

Chapter Preface

Terrorists attack differently than armies do. Armies wear uniforms, attack in large groups, and rely upon large and expensive military equipment. In contrast, terrorists work in small groups, do not wear identifying uniforms, and do not rely upon complex and expensive weapons such as battleships, tanks, and fighter jets. These fundamental differences influence the way terrorists attack.

Resources available to terrorist groups determine how terrorists might attack. Although terrorists have expressed interest in unconventional weapons, such as nuclear or biological devices, according to most experts they have taken only limited steps to pursue them. Bruce Hoffman, author of *Inside Terrorism*, noted that studies of past terrorist behavior suggest that terrorist groups generally prefer basic technologies—"guns and bombs"—and comparatively simple operations. They do so out of a conservative view of technology and a desire that their operations succeed. Also, simpler weapons are cheaper and relatively easy to obtain and use.

Guns are available in many countries without too many restrictions. American gun manufacturers alone produce around 4.5 million guns per year. Weapons far more powerful than handguns or rifles are available on the black market. For example, in August 2007, authorities stumbled upon a Mafia transaction involving a hundred thousand Russian-made automatic weapons. Explosives have even greater potential to kill and terrorize large numbers of people and destroy property. Terrorists often become expert at creating improvised explosive devices that are relatively inexpensive to produce but have a large impact.

In 2008, researchers for the British television program *Dispatches* and the London newspaper the *Evening Standard* blew a six-foot hole in the side of an aircraft fuselage, using only materials that can be carried openly through airport security. The research was prompted by a foiled London attack in 2006 in which terrorists planned to destroy commercial aircraft by mixing together explosive chemical substances while aboard the planes. According to intelligence expert Abdul Hameed Bakier, "the chemicals necessary to create such explosions are easily obtainable. More concerning, however, is the fact that the technical information on how to create such explosives is accessible on many jihadi forums and websites. The most significant and frequently discussed subjects in the jihadi forums are topics pertinent to military tactics and how to create deadly explosives." The *Dispatches* and *Evening Standard* investigation reported that the explosive used in their investigation was made by mixing two easily obtainable chemicals that can be carried through security in containers. The chemicals are inexpensive, odorless, and colorless, and could be easily disguised as toiletries.

Terrorists have less money to fund attacks than do armies, so they must be more resourceful. A United States fighter jet can cost $16 billion dollars. In contrast, the attacks of 9/11, the most elaborate and deadly terrorist attack to date, cost under $350,000. Terrorists were able to use box-cutters to hijack the airplanes and then used the airplanes themselves as missiles to destroy their intended targets. Brian A. Jackson and David R. Frelinger, analysts at the Rand Corporation, have observed that the complex infrastructure systems that make much of modern life possible in America present not just potential targets for attack, but also tools terrorist groups might exploit to cause harm.

Another distinctive feature of terrorism as a mode of warfare is the target of the terrorist attack. Armies target other armies and their weaponry, communications systems, and support facilities. Terrorists, on the other hand, tend to choose "soft," or undefended, targets that have psychological impact and high potential for civilian casualties. According to the National Strategy for Homeland Security, 2006, "Al-Qaida's plotting against our Homeland . . . focuses on prominent political, economic, and infrastructure targets designed to produce mass casualties, visually dramatic destruction, significant economic damage, fear, and loss of confidence in government among our population." The 9/11 attacks combined soft targets with high psychological impact—the World Trade Center and the Pentagon—and mass casualties.

The authors of the following chapter's viewpoints present the debate how susceptible society is to the threat of terrorism.

> *"A nuclear attack on America in the de-*
> *cade ahead is more likely than not."*

Nuclear Terrorism Is a Threat

Graham Allison

In the following viewpoint, Graham Allison argues that nuclear terrorism is a significant threat to America and other countries. According to Allison, nuclear weapons stolen or missing could fall into the hands of terrorists or be provided by countries sympathetic to the terrorists' cause. Or terrorists could make their own weapons, he maintains, if they acquire uranium and basic technical knowledge. The author posits that the terrorist group al Qaeda is committed to killing millions of Americans, and a nuclear weapon would be the best way to achieve that goal. Graham Allison is the founding dean of Harvard's John F. Kennedy School of Government and the director of the Belfer Center for Science and International Affairs.

As you read, consider the following questions:

1. How many "suitcase" nuclear weapons did Russian general Alexander Lebed say were unaccounted for in his country, according to the author?

2. What countries does Allison suggest might provide nuclear weapons to terrorists?

3. According to the author, how many Americans does al Qaeda claim it has the right to kill?

In the weeks and months following 9/11, the American national security community focused on what was called the question of the "second shoe." No one believed that the attacks on the World Trade Center and the Pentagon were an isolated occurrence. The next question had to be when, and where, the second shoe would drop and what form it would take. From the inner circle of presidential advisers to a thick network of external consultants, the nation's best analysts examined an array of potential terrorist attacks, or "horribles." Earlier in the 1990s, when I served as an assistant secretary of defense, I prepared a highly classified memorandum, titled "A Hundred Horribles," that provoked some controversy. On that list, an attack by hijacked aircraft on trophy buildings fell in the lower half of potential terrorist attacks, ranked in terms of damage to America.

Nuclear Attack Is Greatest Fear

First place on everyone's list goes to an attack with a nuclear bomb on an American city. When Secretary of Homeland Security Tom Ridge [2003–2005] is asked what he worries about when he wakes up at night, he answers in one word: "nuclear." Only a nuclear explosion can kill hundreds of thousands of people instantly. But everyone's list also includes other associated forms of nuclear terror, like attacks on nuclear power plants and so-called dirty bombs.

The American Airlines flight that struck the North Tower of the World Trade Center could just as readily have hit the Indian Point nuclear power plant, forty miles north of Times Square. The United Airlines flight that crashed in Pennsylvania on its way to the Capitol might instead have targeted

Three Mile Island. The airplane that attacked the Pentagon could have targeted the North Anna power plant near Richmond, Virginia. At the Counterterrorism Center, analysts recalled that in November 1972, three Americans with pistols and hand grenades hijacked Southern Airways Flight 49. The pilot was ordered to fly to Oak Ridge, Tennessee, where the plane circled over a nuclear research reactor. When the hijackers' ransom demands received a lukewarm response, they forced the pilot to begin a steep descent on Oak Ridge, pulling up only when the airline said it would give the hijackers $2 million. That incident ended in Cuba with the imprisonment of the hijackers.

Consequences of Attacking a Nuclear Plant

The consequences of an attack on a nuclear plant would depend largely on where the plane hit. If the aircraft penetrated the containment dome, the attack could cause the reactor to melt down, releasing hundreds of millions of curies of radioactivity into the surrounding environment, hundreds of times that released by the Hiroshima and Nagasaki atomic bombs. We already know what such an incident would look like. In April 1986, an accidental explosion inside the Soviet nuclear reactor at Chernobyl (near Kiev, in what is now Ukraine) ignited a powerful fire that raged for ten days. The resulting radiation forced the evacuation and resettlement of over 350,000 people and caused an estimated $300 billion of economic damage, and is likely to lead ultimately to tens of thousands of excess cancer deaths among those exposed to the fallout.

An even more vulnerable target at a nuclear plant is the building that houses the spent fuel rods, which are stored in pools of water to prevent the heat from their residual radioactivity from melting them. Designed to remain intact in case of an earthquake, these structures are open to the air in some instances and housed in only light-duty buildings in others, which means that a plane attacking from above might drain

73

the pool, destroy backup safety systems, and ignite the fuel. The resulting fire would spew radioactivity into the environment in amounts that could reach three or four Chernobyls.

Dirty Bombs

Further potential "second shoes" include dirty bombs, conventional explosives packed into radioactive material. While such bombs do not produce a nuclear explosion, they can disperse radiological material over a large area, causing widespread contamination. The consensus in the national security community has long been that a dirty bomb attack is inevitable, indeed long overdue. The integration of various forms of radioactive material in modern life, from X-rays in dentists' offices and hospitals to smoke detectors, has made control of such material impossible. Prior to 9/11, the U.S. government had no serious program even to account for and track the more dangerous materials. Thus newspapers carry almost weekly stories of theft of radioactive material, not only in Russia and the former Soviet Union but here at home as well.

The good news about dirty bombs is that they are weapons of mass disruption, not mass destruction. Potential radiation bombs cover a spectrum from a stick of dynamite in a shoe box containing weak radioactive material to aerosolized plutonium injected into the ventilation system of a skyscraper or an enclosed sports arena. While the former could create temporary panic, the latter could give lung cancer to everyone on an entire floor of a skyscraper. Experts at Los Alamos National Laboratory who studied this threat concluded that "a RDD [radiological dispersal device] attack somewhere in the world is overdue." But as one national security official related, if a radiological dispersal device was the best shot Al Qaeda could now take, we should declare victory.

Nuclear Terrorism Is Most Urgent Threat

Polls taken in 2003 found that four out of every ten Americans say that they "often worry about the chances of a nuclear

Nuclear Terrorism Is Not Hype

"It's not hype. It's something we deal with day in and day out," [FBI director Robert] Mueller said. "When you are talking about an improvised nuclear device, it is something that would be horrifying if it fell into the hands of terrorists or terrorists were able to manufacture such a device."

CBS News, June 13, 2007. www.cbsnews.com.

attack by terrorists." Are these fears exaggerated? Not in the best judgment of those who have carefully examined the evidence. In 2000, two of the most respected and thoughtful Americans who had no previous responsibility in this arena, Howard Baker and Lloyd Cutler, conducted an official review of this issue. Baker, a Republican, is currently the U.S. ambassador to Japan, having served previously as President Ronald Reagan's chief of staff and as majority leader of the Senate. Cutler, a Democrat, has been counsel to the president in both the [Jimmy] Carter and the [Bill] Clinton administrations. The principal finding of the Report Card they presented to the [George W.] Bush administration in January 2001 states bluntly: "The *most urgent unmet national security threat* to the United States today is the danger that weapons of mass destruction or weapons-usable material in Russia could be stolen, sold to terrorists or hostile nation-states and used against American troops abroad or citizens at home." As Baker testified to the Senate Foreign Relations Committee: "It really boggles my mind that there could be 40,000 nuclear weapons, or maybe 80,000, in the former Soviet Union, poorly controlled and poorly stored, and that the world isn't in a near state of hysteria about the danger."

Theft of Nuclear Weapons

The imminence of this threat becomes evident as one considers three points. First, thefts of weapons-usable material and attempts to steal nuclear weapons are not a hypothetical possibility, but a proven and recurring fact. Thousands of weapons and tens of thousands of potential weapons (softball-size lumps of highly enriched uranium and plutonium) remain today in unsecured storage facilities in Russia, vulnerable to theft by determined criminals who could then sell them to terrorists. In the years since the collapse of the Soviet Union, there have been hundreds of confirmed cases of successful theft of nuclear materials in which the thieves were captured, sometimes in Russia, on other occasions in the Czech Republic, Germany, and elsewhere. Every month those who follow current events closely will learn of yet another occasion in which nuclear material was stolen or a theft attempted.

In 1997, [then-Russian president] Boris Yeltsin's assistant for national security affairs, General Alexander Lebed, acknowledged that 84 of some 132 special KGB "suitcase" nuclear weapons were not accounted for in Russia. These weapons are miniature nuclear devices (0.1 to 1 kiloton), small enough to fit into a suitcase carried by a single individual. Under pressure from colleagues, Lebed later recanted his statement, retreating to the official Russian line that the Soviet Union had never made any such nuclear weapons; that it was inconceivable that Russia could have lost a nuclear weapon; and that, in any case, all such Russian weapons and nuclear materials were secure. But in the process, Lebed and his colleagues left more questions than answers. Contrary to the Russian government's claims, there can be no doubt about the fact that enough nuclear material to build more than twenty nuclear weapons was lost in the transition from the Soviet Union to Russia. Indeed, over one thousand pounds of highly enriched uranium (HEU) was purchased by the U.S. government, removed from an unprotected site in Almaty, Kazakhstan, and is now securely stored in Oak Ridge. But, as former CIA director John Deutch observed, "It's not so much what I know that worries me, as what I know that I don't know."

Terrorists Could Obtain Uranium

Second, in the winter of 2002–2003, President Bush argued that "if the Iraqi regime is able to produce, buy, or steal an amount of uranium a little bigger than a softball, it could have a nuclear weapon in less than a year," a charge that served as part of his case for war with Iraq. What the president failed to mention is that with the same quantity of HEU, terrorist groups like Al Qaeda, Hezbollah, and Hamas could do the same thing. The only high hurdle to creating a nuclear bomb is access to fissionable material—an ingredient that is, fortunately, difficult and expensive to manufacture. But as John Foster, a leading American bomb maker and former director of the Lawrence Livermore National Laboratories, wrote a quarter century ago, "If the essential nuclear materials are at hand, it is possible to make an atomic bomb using information that is available in the open literature."

Third, terrorists would not find it difficult to smuggle such a nuclear device into the United States. The nuclear material in question is smaller than a football. Even an assembled device, like a suitcase nuclear weapon, could be sent in a Federal Express package, shipped in a cargo container, or checked as airline baggage. Of the seven million cargo containers that arrive in U.S. ports each year, fewer than 5 percent are opened for inspection. As the chief executive of CSX Lines, one of the foremost container-shipping companies, noted, "If you can smuggle heroin in containers, you may be able to smuggle in a nuclear bomb."

Unfortunately, the former Soviet Union is not the only potential source of nuclear weapons or fissile material from which a nuclear weapon could be fashioned. Pakistan has an arsenal of about fifty nuclear weapons and materials for making at least that many more. Given the extensive ties between Pakistani intelligence services and the Taliban, it is not unreasonable to envision Pakistan as the source of a ten-kiloton weapon in New York. Unfolding revelations about fissile material production lines in North Korea, Iran, and Libya lengthen the list for potential sources of the first nuclear terrorist's weapon.

Easy to Make Nuclear Weapons

After Tom Clancy published *The Sum of All Fears*, his 1991 best-seller about a stolen nuclear weapon being detonated at the Super Bowl, the author received comments from several knowledgeable insiders that left him uneasy. Thus the paperback edition of the book includes a remarkable afterword written, as Clancy confesses candidly, "to salve my conscience, *not* in my reasonable expectation that it matters a damn."

> All of the material in this novel relating to weapons technology and fabrication is readily available in any one of dozens of books. . . . I was first bemused, then stunned, as my research revealed just how easy such a project might be today. It is generally known that nuclear secrets are not as secure as we would like—in fact, the situation is worse than even well-informed people appreciate. What required billions of dollars in the 1940s is much less expensive today. A modern personal computer has far more power and reliability than the first Eniac, and the "hydrocodes" which enable a computer to test and validate a weapon's design are easily duplicated. The exquisite machine tools used to fabricate parts can be had for the asking. When I asked explicitly for specifications for the very machines used at Oak Ridge and elsewhere, they arrived Federal Express the next day. Some highly specialized items designed specifically for bomb manufacture may now be found in stereo speakers. The fact of the matter is that a sufficiently wealthy individual could,

over a period of from five to ten years, produce a multistage thermonuclear device. Science is all in the public domain, and allows few secrets.

Clancy wrote this afterword in 1992, which means his five- to ten-year period has elapsed.

The Right to Kill Four Million Americans

Nine months after the attack on New York, Osama bin Laden's official press spokesman, Suleiman Abu Gheith, made a chilling announcement on a now defunct Al Qaeda-associated Web site, www.alneda.com. "*We have the right,*" Abu Gheith asserted, "*to kill 4 million Americans—2 million of them children—and to exile twice as many and wound and cripple hundred of thousands.*"

Four million Americans—an eerily specific and precise figure, clearly not one pulled out of thin air. More troubling than Abu Gheith's number is the logic, and even the bizarre coherence, of the calculations that led Al Qaeda to this stark conclusion. In an extended, three-part article, Abu Gheith explains "why we fight the United States" and seeks to provide "the Islamic justification for Al Qaeda's jihad against the U.S." The bottom line of the case he makes for Al Qaeda members and affiliates around the world is four million dead Americans.

About the attacks on the World Trade Center, he proclaims, "What happened to America is something natural, an expected event for a country that uses terror, arrogant policy, and suppression against the nations and peoples, and imposes a single method, thought, and way of life, as if the people of the entire world are clerks in its government offices and employed by the commercial companies and institutions. Anyone who was surprised, did not understand the nature of man and the effects of oppression and tyranny on man's emotions and feelings." Echoing a phrase used by Palestinian militants to characterize Israel's tactics in the West Bank and Gaza, he says, "They thought that oppression begets surrender."

Why target the United States? His answer is clear: "America with the collaboration of the Jews is the leader of corruption and the breakdown of values, whether moral, ideological, political, or economic corruption. It disseminates abomination and licentiousness among the people via the cheap media and the vile curricula." In sum, "America is the reason for all oppression, injustice, licentiousness, or suppression that is the Muslim's lot. It stands behind all the disasters that were caused and are still being caused to the Muslims; it is immersed in the blood of Muslims and can not hide this."

Abu Gheith's indictment then itemizes deaths and injuries the United States and Israel have (in his view) caused Muslims:

- For fifty years in Palestine, the Jews—with the blessing and support of the Americans—carried out abominations of murder, suppression, abuse, and exile. The Jews exiled nearly 5 million Palestinians and killed nearly 260,000. They wounded nearly 180,000 and crippled nearly 160,000.

- As a result of the American bombings and siege of Iraq, more than 1.2 million Muslims were killed in the past decade. Due to the siege, over one million children are killed annually; that is 83,333 children on average per month, 2,777 children per day. (This refers to the sanctions and enforcement of UN resolutions *before* the American-led invasion in 2003.)

- In its war against the Taliban and Al Qaeda in Afghanistan, America killed 12,000 Afghan civilians and 350 Arab jihad fighters.

- In Somalia, America killed 13,000 Somalis.

Religion Requires Mass Deaths

How should honorable Muslims respond? he asks. Citing the Koran and other Islamic religious texts and traditions, he answers that "anyone who peruses these sources reaches a single conclusion: the sages have agreed that the reciprocal punishment to which the verses referred is not limited to a specific instance. It is a valid rule for punishments for infidels, for the licentious Muslims, and for the oppressors."

In conclusion, "according to the numbers in the previous section of the lives lost among Muslims because of the Americans, directly or indirectly," therefore, "we are still at the beginning of the way. The Americans have still not tasted from our hands what we have tasted from theirs. We have not reached parity with them." For Al Qaeda, "parity will require killing 4 million Americans." For, according to Abu Gheith, "America knows only the language of force. This is the only way to make it take its hands off the Muslims. America can be kept at bay by blood alone."

Nearly three thousand Americans died in the 9/11 attacks. It would take 1,400 similar assaults to reach that figure of 4 million. Or it could take just one, if Al Qaeda had access to the right nuclear weapon. Al Qaeda has made its intentions clear; the challenge to America is to prevent it from succeeding.

We Can Prevent Nuclear Terrorism

The world's most successful investor is also a legendary odds maker in pricing insurance policies for unlikely but catastrophic events like earthquakes. Warren Buffett has described a nuclear terrorist attack as "the ultimate depressing thing. It will happen. It's inevitable. I don't see any way that it won't happen." Given the number of actors with serious intent, the accessibility of weapons or nuclear materials from which elementary weapons could be constructed, and the almost limitless ways in which terrorists could smuggle a weapon through

American borders, a betting person would have to go with Buffett. In my own considered judgment, on the current path, a nuclear terrorist attack on America in the decade ahead is more likely than not.

And yet I am not a pessimist. The central but largely unrecognized truth is that nuclear terrorism is *preventable*. As a simple matter of physics, without fissile material, there can be no nuclear explosion. There is a vast, but not unlimited, amount of highly enriched uranium and weapons-grade plutonium in the world, and it is within our power to keep it secure. The United States does not lose gold from Fort Knox, nor Russia treasures from the Kremlin Armory. Thus all that the United States and its allies have to do to prevent nuclear terrorism is to prevent terrorists from acquiring a weapon or nuclear material. The "all" required calls for a substantial, sustained, but nonetheless finite undertaking that can be accomplished by a finite effort. It is a challenge to our will, our conviction, and our courage, not to our technical capacity.

> *"The prospects for developing a practical nuclear terrorist option in the near future [are] practically nil."*

The Threat of Nuclear Terrorism Is Exaggerated

James W. Moore

In the following viewpoint, James W. Moore argues that the threat of nuclear terrorism has been greatly exaggerated. While a nuclear device could kill millions, he asserts, few terrorist groups have that as a goal. Moore also states that the availability of nuclear material on the black market is greatly exaggerated. Building a nuclear device requires considerable technical resources and knowledge that terrorists do not have, he says, adding that if terrorists were able to build a nuclear device, they would have done so already. James W. Moore is a senior strategic analyst with the Department of National Defence in Canada.

As you read, consider the following questions:

1. In Moore's view, what terrorist group is the only one with motivation to carry out a nuclear attack?

James W. Moore, "Nuclear Terrorism: Exaggerating the Threat?" *The Journal of Conflict Studies*, vol. 26, no. 1, Summer 2006. Reproduced by permission.

2. According to Moore, the total amount of highly-enriched uranium available on the black market between 1993 and 2004 is what percentage of the amount needed to build a gun-type improvised nuclear device?

3. In the author's view, when was the ideal time for al Qaeda to have built a nuclear device if they were capable of doing so?

The 11 September terrorist attacks on the World Trade Center and Pentagon were a devastating "wake-up call" for the United States, bringing home to Americans as never before the dangers of transnational terrorism. It also opened the eyes of many to the risk of a far more perilous danger—the threat of nuclear terrorist attack. As the *National Security Strategy of the United States of America* warned in March 2006, "[t]here are few greater threats than a terrorist attack with WMD [weapons of mass destruction]."

In 2005, two comprehensive studies of the nuclear terrorist threat were published: Graham Allison's *Nuclear Terrorism: The Ultimate Preventable Catastrophe* and Charles Ferguson, et al.'s *The Four Faces of Nuclear Terrorism*. These two studies examine the threat that nuclear terrorism poses in the post-11 September world and then set out a series of policy recommendations intended to reduce if not eliminate altogether the risk of a catastrophic nuclear terrorist attack. The theme of these two studies is the same. In *Nuclear Terrorism*, Allison argues bluntly that a terrorist attack against a US city using a nuclear weapon is inevitable but also preventable if essential measures to safeguard nuclear weapons and materials are urgently taken. Though not as categorical as Allison, Ferguson, et al. in *The Four Faces* agree that, while nuclear terrorism has threatened the US for many years, "this peril looms larger today than ever before." . . .

An Exaggerated Threat

The argument of this essay is, basically, that the threat of this particular strand of nuclear terrorism as presented in these two studies is greatly exaggerated.

One must hasten to strongly emphasize that this does *not* mean that the threat is insignificant, nor that it is one that can be casually ignored or dismissed. This author agrees wholeheartedly with Allison and Ferguson, et al. that there is no room for complacency regarding the nuclear terrorist threat. The acquisition or construction of a nuclear weapon by terrorists is a sufficiently serious prospect if only because of the catastrophic consequences should such a device be used to warrant urgent action to reduce the danger. Nevertheless, their tendency to exaggerate the magnitude of the threat—in order to pierce the complacency that they argue permeates US government actions when it comes to instituting needed national and international nuclear control measures—has the unintended consequence of distracting attention from the very measures that need to be taken. Extreme threats beget extreme solutions. Rather than prompting government officials to act with dispatch on the more mundane but essential policy actions needed to secure nuclear materials and weapons worldwide, the exaggerated threat of nuclear terrorism only encourages and sustains more extreme domestic and international policies in the global war on terror, such as warrantless domestic wiretapping and preventive counterproliferation war. In the final analysis, exaggeration does more harm than good. . . .

Motivation for Nuclear Terrorism

Who might engage in nuclear terrorism? Ferguson, et al. provide a largely theoretical examination of the incentives and disincentives that could motivate terrorist groups to seek to construct and use an IND [improvised nuclear device]. They describe these motivations in the context of four archetypal terrorist groups:

- Apocalyptic groups—groups striving to precipitate the end of the world through catalytic, catastrophic violence, e.g., *Aum Shinrikyo* [a destructive, doomsday religious cult centered in Japan].

- Politico-religious groups—hybrid groups combining political and religious motivations, e.g., *al-Qaeda* and *Hezbollah*.

- Traditional national/separatist groups—groups focusing on achieving political objectives for a specific ethnic or tribal group, e.g., the IRA [Irish Republican Army] and Tamil Tigers [a militant nationalist organization seeking an independent Tamil state in Sri Lanka].

- Single-issue groups—groups opposing clearly defined social or political policies, e.g., animal liberation, anti-abortion and anti-nuclear groups.

One motivation for building an IND common to virtually all these terrorist groups, the authors maintain, would be the acquisition of a capability with which to blackmail or deter their opponents. The threat or use of such a capability would demonstrate a group's capability and power, and tremendously enhance its prestige both among its allies and enemies. Beyond that, Ferguson, et al. argue that the incentives depend upon the type of terrorist organization. An apocalyptic group, for example, might see an IND as the means to spark a nuclear conflagration that would bring about the end of the world. A politico-religious group might view an IND as an ideal weapon with which to carry out its strategy of inflicting maximum harm—physical, economic, and psychological—upon the enemy. A traditional national/separatist group, on the other hand, might consider the possession rather than the actual use of an IND as most useful in terms of enhancing its prestige, potentially bringing it international recognition, and allowing it to feign the attributes of statehood. Conversely, a single-issue anti-nuclear group is unlikely, in their estimation, to find an IND useful as such a group's focus would not be on mass destruction but on exposing the dangers of nuclear technology.

Few Terrorist Groups Want Nukes

The authors recognize that the balance sheet on nuclear terrorism is not all positive from the terrorists' standpoint. Implementation challenges, e.g., acquiring the fissile material and retaining the technological expertise needed to construct an IND might dissuade some terrorist groups from pursuing this avenue. Moreover, nuclear terrorism itself presents new problems, challenges, and demands on terrorist organizations, requiring an organizational culture of innovation and individual initiative. However, most terrorist groups, they note, tend to be conservative in orientation, staying with conventional methods of attack that are "tried and true."

Taking all these incentives and disincentives into account, Ferguson, et al. conclude that few terrorist groups have the motivation or capabilities to attempt some form of nuclear terrorism. In their estimation, *al-Qaeda* is likely the only network with the requisite characteristics to pursue extreme nuclear terror either by acquiring or developing a nuclear weapon. . . .

Allison's arguments for an expansive "rogue's gallery" of potential nuclear terrorism perpetrators, at least in the case of Hezbollah, are unpersuasive. He fails to demonstrate that, apart from *al-Qaeda*, there are other terrorist groups who live only to kill Americans and are "chomping at the bit" to acquire and use nuclear weapons against US targets. Ferguson, et al.'s conclusion that *al-Qaeda* is likely the only terrorist network with the motivation to carry out such an attack is much more realistic. Indeed, it is enough to know that *al-Qaeda* has demonstrated an active interest in acquiring nuclear weapons to drive home the magnitude of the nuclear terrorist threat.

Suitcase Nukes Do Not Exist

Members of Congress have warned about the dangers of suitcase nuclear weapons. Hollywood has made television shows and movies about them. Even the Federal Emergency Management Agency has alerted Americans to a threat—information the White House includes on its Web site.

But government experts and intelligence officials say such a threat gets vastly more attention than it deserves. These officials said a true suitcase nuke would be highly complex to produce, require significant upkeep and cost a small fortune. . . .

"The suitcase nuke is an exciting topic that really lends itself to movies," said Vahid Majidi, the assistant director of the FBI's Weapons of Mass Destruction Directorate. "No one has been able to truly identify the existence of these devices."

Katharine Schrader, Associated Press, November 10, 2007.

There is no need to exaggerate the list of potential perpetrators in order to make the point that there are terrorists out there with a deeply troubling interest in nuclear weapons. . . .

Nuclear Material Not Available

Allison and Ferguson, et al. give the impression that there exists a thriving black market in nuclear material, a virtual "Home Depot" for "do-it-yourself" nuclear bomb makers. In fact, the black market in fissile material is tiny and undeveloped. In 1995, the International Atomic Energy Agency (IAEA) established the Illicit Trafficking Database (ITDB) in order to track the "unauthorized acquisition, provision, possession, use, transfer, or disposal of nuclear materials and other radioactive materials, whether intentional or unintentional and with or without crossing international borders, including unsuccessful and thwarted events." According to the ITDB, as of 31 December 2004, there were 662 confirmed incidents of trafficking in radioactive sources. Of these, only 18 involved nuclear materials that "could be a shortcut to nuclear proliferation and to nuclear terrorism." The ITDB notes that, of these 18, only a few involved more than small quantities of weapons-grade material. Indeed, the cumulative amounts of highly enriched uranium and plutonium involved in all 18 incidents total only 8.521 kg and .373 kg, respectively. To put this in perspective. Ferguson, et al. estimate that terrorists would need 40 to 50 kg of weapons-grade HEU [highly enriched uranium] to have reasonable confidence that a simple gun-type IND would work. They could cut back on the required amount of fissile material if they can master the more technically challenging implosion-type design. In such a design, roughly 25 kg of weapons-grade HEU or 8 kg of plutonium are needed. Tallying up all the weapons-grade fissile material that has "flooded" onto the nuclear black market from 1993 to 2004, we find that this material amounts to 17 percent to 21 percent of the HEU needed to build a gun-type IND, and 34 percent and 5 percent of the material needed to build, respectively, an HEU or plutonium implosion-type bomb.

On this basis it is difficult to argue convincingly that there is a "thriving" market in fissile material just waiting to supply terrorists with their nuclear material needs. Of course, what is of greatest concern is what we do not know about the nuclear black market. Testifying before the House Subcommittee on Prevention of Nuclear and Biological Attack, Rensselaer Lee, an authority on the nuclear black market in the FSU [former Soviet Union] and Europe, observed that "[l]ittle nuclear material of significance and no nuclear warheads appear to circulate in the black market; buyers are elusive; and arrest and seizure statistics provide little evidence of participation in the market by rogue states, terrorists, and major transnational crime formations." However, Lee warns, this may be a "misleading guide" to the true dimensions of the nuclear market. Like the illicit drug trade, what we see may be only the tip of the black market iceberg. He argues that "some significant incidents go unreported, particularly in the former Soviet states. Also, it stands to reason that sophisticated and well-connected smugglers are far less likely to get caught than the amateur criminals and scam artists who dominate the known incidents."

Critics do not find Lee's arguments convincing. Robin Frost, a Canadian government analyst specializing in nuclear proliferation, maintains that "[t]o argue that a large black market exists, and that the failure to detect it is proof of the fiendish cunning of those who operate it, is sophistry of the least persuasive kind." . . .

Terrorists Lack Know-How

To surmount the technical challenges in designing and assembling an IND a terrorist group would have to bring together a small team knowledgeable in nuclear physics or engineering, metallurgy, machining, draftsmanship, conventional explosives, and chemical processing. A well-financed terrorist network such as *al-Qaeda*, the authors assert, would probably have little difficulty in recruiting people with the required skills. For example, it could attract sympathetic scientists from Pakistan, Iran, Iraq, and/or Russia, though in the case of Russia there is no evidence to date that it has succeeded in this effort. The authors concur with Allison's assessment that a team of a dozen specialists would take roughly one year to assemble a workable device. Again, like Allison, they consider the greater challenge for aspiring nuclear terrorists to be acquiring the requisite fissile material, not the actual construction of a gun-type nuclear device, which they describe as "relatively simple."

Are Allison and Ferguson, et al. correct in their assertion that the recipe for a crude but workable IND is "out there"? A closer look at some of the information that Allison and Ferguson, et al. maintain is readily available to aspiring nuclear terrorists through the Internet and other sources reveals that these sources present the *basic design principles* of nuclear weapons. They do not provide precise details on the construction of such weapons. For example, Allison observes that "The H-Bomb Secret" published in *Progressive* magazine describes the physics of the hydrogen bomb in detail, complete with schematics of a thermonuclear weapon. The article does, in fact, provide such schematics. However, these schematics are only simplified diagrams illustrating the basic design principles of such a weapon. As J. Carson Mark and four co-authors, all former US nuclear weapons designers, noted in a 1986 article, "[s]chematic drawings of fission explosive devices of the earliest types showing in a qualitative way the principles used in achieving the first fission explosions are widely available. However, the detailed design drawings and specifications that are essential before it is possible to plan the fabrication of actual parts are not available." These basic design schematics are not the blueprints for a bomb.

However, Mark, et al. wrote their seminal article over 20 years ago. Has the situation changed since then? In particular, do the disclosures regarding Libya's WMD program suggest that detailed blueprints for a nuclear weapon are now circulating on the black market? These blueprints appear to be the most complete design information available outside of official state nuclear establishments. The documents, which Tripoli turned over to US officials in November 2003, "contained detailed, step-by-step instructions for assembling [a 1,000-lb.] implosion-type nuclear bomb that could fit atop a large ballistic missile. They also included technical instructions for manufacturing components for the device." However, even these extensive blueprints were apparently incomplete. While they included most essential design elements, officials and experts who examined the "hodgepodge" of documents noted that "*a few key parts were missing* [emphasis added]. . . . Some investigators have speculated that the missing papers could have been lost, or hadn't yet been provided—possibly they were being withheld pending additional payments." It would seem that Mark, et al.'s conclusion from 20 years still holds true today: a *complete* recipe detailing the steps from A to Z for building an IND is not available in the public domain.

Myths About Building a Bomb

In other words working with the basic design information that is already available terrorists would still need to "take it to the next level" in terms of preparing detailed blueprints for a workable IND. But is this such a challenging task? Allison highlights the case of a Princeton aerospace major, John Aristotle Phillips, who over a period of *five months* in 1977, designed an implosion-type bomb from publicly available information for his senior thesis. According to Allison, "the resulting design was a perfect terrorist weapon: a bomb the size of a beach ball, with a ten-kiloton yield and a price tag of $2,000." The physics faculty at the university concluded that the design would work and the US government subsequently classified the thesis as "secret." This suggests that designing a nuclear device is a relatively simple matter, well within the capabilities of even a university undergraduate student. And yet, Ferguson, et al. note that Iraqi nuclear weapons scientists required *several years* to develop a workable nuclear weapon design based on the same implosion principle.

What are we to make of this apparent discrepancy? Is it possible that the "native ingenuity" of an American undergraduate student so far exceeds the skills and expertise of Iraqi nuclear scientists that he was able to come up with a workable weapons design on his own in a fraction of the time that a team of professional scientists needed over three years to produce? More likely, Phillips's thesis presented broad design principles which, though a major step forward on the path to a workable nuclear device, fell well short of the precise engineering specifications needed to actually construct such a weapon. Or it could be that his design was basically wrong. Whatever the case, Allison's claim that "the implosion design now lies within the grasp of undergraduate science majors" is a gross overstatement that only perpetuates the mythology that has sprung up around the Phillips case. . . .

Why Has *al-Qaeda* Not Built a Bomb?

Even if we were to grant Allison's contention that a nuclear terrorist attack is inevitable, this still leaves one nagging question that both studies conspicuously fail to address. If terrorists are fanatically committed to acquiring and using a nuclear weapon, if fissile material for a bomb is easily available, and if construction of a crude IND is so simple, why have they not built and used a nuclear device before now? With respect to al-Qaeda, the conditions for such an endeavor would seem to have been ideal during the 1990s. As the RAND report points out, *al-Qaeda* had a number of advantages working in its favor during this period:

- Financial—possibly hundreds of millions of US$;

- Sanctuary—Sudan, then Afghanistan;

- Organizational capacity—front companies endowed him [bin Laden] with seemingly legitimate logistical and financial means;

- Demonstrated operational capacities by simultaneously attacking separate targets in different countries;

- Some technical expertise. Why, then, did *al-Qaeda* not capitalize on these advantages to construct an IND? More importantly, why did it fritter away the element of strategic surprise with the 11 September attacks?

Al-Qaeda has demonstrated an impressive degree of organizational patience, inserting sleeper cells in target societies to be activated years down the road, and patiently planning terrorist attacks over periods of months and years. It publicly acknowledges that it is in this battle with the "infidel" for the long run. Why, then, did it not wait until it had completed construction of an IND before awakening the US "sleeping giant" and losing many of these advantages in Washington's retaliatory action following 11 September?

Nuclear Terrorism Not Practical

Possibly, it was a case of miscalculation on the part of *al-Qaeda's* leadership. From an operational standpoint bin Laden and his cohorts may not have anticipated the dramatic destruction that the 11 September attacks would inflict. From a strategic standpoint bin Laden may also have underestimated the reaction of the Bush administration to the attacks. The lukewarm response of the Clinton administration to previous terrorist attacks during the 1990s may have led him to believe that Washington would refrain once again from severe and sustained retaliation in response to the attack. On the other hand Washington's response in striking back . . . with the invasion and occupation of Afghanistan and Iraq may have been the exact response that bin Laden was hoping to provoke in order to mobilize the Islamic masses against the West and its client apostate regimes, and to facilitate attacks against the elements of US power.

However, it could very well be that the "premature" attacks on 11 September were carried out because the prospects for developing a practical nuclear terrorist option in the near future were practically nil. Contrary to the arguments in *Nuclear Terrorism* and *The Four Faces*, essential fissile material may not be so readily available on the black market, and building an IND from basic design principles may be harder than is thought, especially for a terrorist network that lacks the essential scientific and technical expertise needed to execute the project. Though Allison and Ferguson, et al. may see the perpetration of nuclear terrorism as inevitable, the view may be very different from the terrorists' "side of the fence."

> *"Terrorists already use, and will inten-*
> *sify the inherent potential use of the*
> *internet as a powerful destructive*
> *weapon."*

Cyberterrorism Is a Serious Threat

Sam Elrom

In the following viewpoint, Sam Elrom argues that cyberterrorists will strike at some point in the United States. Both government and business are dependent on the Internet, he says, making the network an ideal target for a terrorist attack. According to Elrom, cyberterrorists are becoming more skillful and have initiated some attacks on specific targets to learn how networks detect and respond to such strikes. He adds that "E-jihadists," distribute programs that can be used to overwhelm the servers of Web sites. The author concludes that experts who claim cyberterror is not a threat are underestimating terrorists' desire and capabilities. Sam Elrom is president of a security consulting firm specializing in defense, intelligence, and technological security analysis.

Sam Elrom, "Dark Web Terror—the Threat That Got Lost in Traffic—Part Two," *The Elrom Report*, November 30, 2006. http://theelromreport.com. Reproduced by permission.

As you read, consider the following questions:

1. According to Elrom, what would be the economic cost to business and e-commerce if there was a twenty-four-hour crash of the Internet?
2. What trend within the cyberterrorist field does the author say is creating a "buzz" among information technology professionals?
3. What does a jihadist Web site quoted by the author say is the best method and means to inflict maximum human, financial, and morale damage on its enemies?

Surprisingly, the results of a senior IT [information technology] members survey conducted by *Insight IT* magazine in December 2006, show that "eighty-two percent of IT executives believe that a cyber-terrorist attack on U.S. companies is likely to occur in the next five years." Furthermore, the same survey reports that "over half of companies over $1 billion report security breaches in the past 12 months, and 45 percent have been targeted by organized criminals. Penetration by spyware and viruses remain problems, but they're not the only ones: nearly half of all companies that have had security breaches say equipment containing company data has been lost or stolen." This is what they really think, despite fat budgets and layers of protection invested by the companies to protect their system against penetration. Based on this survey and many similar results from repeated polling of IT professionals on this issue, there exists an obvious duality, characterized by an innate disbelief of terrorists' capability to launch a powerful cyber attack in one hand, and the personal conviction and real fear, that such an attack could take place in any given moment.

Cyberterrorists Will Strike

The results support the fact that there is a constant growing threat that terrorists will use a massive cyber attack, as part of a multiple attack strategy. In his thorough description of this threat, Gregory J. Rattray wrote: "Increasingly, cyberterrorists can achieve effects in the US from nearly anywhere on the globe. Terrorist groups can access global information infrastructures owned and operated by the governments and corporations they want to target. Digital attackers have a wide variety of means to cause disruption and/or destruction. Response in kind by the US government against sophisticated attackers is near impossible due to the difficulty of pinpointing activity in cyberspace and legal strictures on tracing attackers."

Furthermore, the renowned historian and terror expert Walter Laquer, observed in his essay "Post Modern Terrorism" as early as September 1996: ". . . why assassinate a politician or indiscriminately kill people when an attack on electronic switching will produce far more dramatic and long-lasting results." The writing was on the wall as early as the mid 90s, but again, nobody saw it, or preferred not to see it.

There is little doubt that the effectiveness of the means that could generate a digital attack continue to increase, meaning that the US will be more vulnerable to cyberterrorism. Terrorists using cyberterrorism have already reached a high degree of sophistication, developing technological attack tools and effective targeting strategies. On the other hand, Rattray points out that "limits to hitting back against cyberterrorism will remain a difficult problem," recognizing that the threat is real, and that we are ill equipped to respond swiftly and decisively.

Internet Dependency

Parallel to the industrial development worldwide and the emergence of new giant economies such as Russia, China and India, to mention just a few, the whole business community, the entire government system and the entire industries, not to mention the private sector and household connected systems, are today totally addicted to instant information which the internet provides. This reliance on information which did not exist only twenty years ago, created a new field of opportunities in which terrorism flourishes. Why? Because as the accessibility to the world wide web becomes more simple and the software more complicated, the easier it is to attack defined targets and bring them down, crashing the whole structure and infrastructure connected to each other. Of course, IT companies, which have an invested interest obviously, IT managers and system administrators, and many in the academia, dismiss the actual threat by pointing out that:

- each system is independent

- redundant systems are in place

- there are emergency plans in case of a catastrophic event

- past experience and special war games have shown that the overall damage would be contained and systems would be reactivated faster than expected

Maybe so, but can anyone imagine a day without the internet and its ramifications [for] the businesses, industries and private users? What would be the price of a sudden business and e-commerce crash that will be sustained for only 24 hours? The answer is: between 17 to 24 billion dollars direct loss. And what would happen if the banking system alone will crash for 24 hours? A loss of approximately 30 billion.

An Ideal Target for Terrorists

It's a well known fact that information is the life blood of commerce. Modern life has bestowed "information," and real-time information specifically, as the most important factor in commerce. More so, is the ability to access it any time, anywhere, transfer, exchange and act upon it, all based on the assumption that the information is accurate, in real time and protected. This demands wider, deeper, faster and more sophisticated networks, an ever-growing infrastructure and a continuous demand for more: more speed, more security, more options and more information. But, we should beware of what we ask for because as the power of the internet and the infrastructure it's based on increases so [do] the chances of non-malicious disruption, or ... a focused terrorist attack on the system. Let alone the financial implications, the psychological impact on the whole Western system would be enormous, not to mention the disastrous impact on the military and security systems.

What is the likelihood of such a catastrophic event to ever unfold? Very high in my opinion, because we've seen the extreme changes in the way terrorists use the internet. . . . It makes perfect sense that the almost total reliance on the internet by business, government, military, academia and society in general, only emphasized what a huge target it became for terrorists to hit. Imagine a simultaneous attack targeting a critical infrastructure site like a nuclear power plant and its supporting and connecting network; beside the physical damage and the psychological effect, the collapse of the communication network may send a shock wave of secondary crashes impacting connected, related and remote networks and locations, which like a delayed earthquake shock create an unstoppable ripple effect. And it is not rocket science to comprehend that from the terrorists' point of view scores of casualties may be the ultimate goal PR [public relations] wise, but financial havoc and business chaos can be more destructive, because it impacts the immediate lives of everybody.

Cyberterrorists Becoming More Skillful

Despite continuous investments in software, network architecture, technology and infrastructure, cyberterrorism has become one of the most hard to protect challenges in combating terrorism.

Cyber Attack Shuts Down Estonia

The Internet is not only the means by which attacks may be planned and executed; it is a target in and of itself. Last April [2007] Estonia suffered what has been called a "cyber blockade." Wave after wave of data requests from computers around the world shut down banks and emergency phone lines, gas stations and grocery stores, newspapers and television stations, even the prime minister's office.

Robert S. Mueller, speech at State College, Pennsylvania, November 6, 2007.

What about redundancy, backup systems, layers of infrastructure protection, etc, one may ask? Well it exists but suffers from unprotected gaps, under-protected sub-systems, lack of periodical and costly software and hardware updated versions, but mostly, lack of IT professionals that understand both the technological and security challenge. Nonetheless, the most critical problem to deal with is that we really don't know what the terrorists' capabilities are. If the development in recent years is an indicator as to the technical and software level and IT development terrorists reached by analyzing their internet activity alone, then we have an undeniable problem on our hands. Another indicator comes from studying how terrorists prepared and launched cyber attacks against selected targets and the results may scare some naysayers.

For example, a new identified trend regarding the rapid development of cyberterror is creating a big buzz lately. Professionals have expressed a growing concern related to the increase in the frequency of attacks on the internet which display a significant augmentation in sophistication and a considerable increase in terrorists' capability to detect and use weak spots in the protective software to attack networks, mainly sites that are aggressively anti-Islamic or anti-Jihad, including Muslims. Serious concerns continue to raise due to the interpretation of what those attacks mean, which is: the complexity and sophistication of the attacks is increasing, yet the attack launchers need lower and less professional skills to successfully produce an effective attack. What this means is that terrorists study every initiated attack and the response to it and learn what works and what doesn't, where were new vulnerabilities detected, what was the local response and what are the methods the attacked network initiated to detect and protect itself.

Reasons Why Cyberterror Attack Will Occur

It's troubling that many experts dismiss the serious threat posed by dark-web cyber attacks, because terrorists already use, and will intensify the inherent potential use of the internet as a powerful destructive weapon. Here is why:

- The count of potential targets is enormous and is growing by the day. Everything becomes a potential target, from private networks, institutions, academia, the military, the banking system, the government, the private business systems, public utilities, airlines, and many others.

- The amount, the variety and the complexity of potential targets ensures that terrorists will find weaknesses and vulnerabilities to exploit.

- The cyber space provides anonymity which is of course welcomed by the terrorists using its methods. Operation-wise, terrorist attackers, like any other user, use screen names and can log on [to] an existing website without the need of identification or a proof of [authorization], making it very difficult for the protective agencies and law enforcement forces to track down the terrorists' real identity.

- Both scientific and practical studies have shown that the entire critical infrastructures, as detailed in the list released by the DHS [Department of Homeland Security], including electric power grids, emergency services, oil and gas pipelines and refineries, the water system, airports and commercial ports, all are vulnerable to a cyberterrorist attack. But not only those systems are exposed; the military and intelligence networks are even more susceptible, although the consensus is that those networks are much better protected. This is a viable threat mainly because the infrastructures and servers/ computer systems that run those networks are very complex and connected with each other in many subtle undetectable ways, making it effectively impossible to eliminate all potential weaknesses, not to mention problems that such systems encounter routinely.

- Terror-based cyber attacks are launched remotely, a very appealing characteristic to terrorists. Not only that, but once triggered a cyberterrorism attack needs no more monitoring, supervision or presence on the web, and the results, if successful, can be heard and seen shortly on all media outlets.

- Cyberterror does not require physical training, only recruiting of well trained IT professionals, which is an easy task. In addition, there is no need of psychological training, there is no physical risk and the chances of being caught are slim anyway, better than other, more dangerous alternatives, and all together easier and more safe.

- There is no need of subsequent investments since everything is virtual, remote and unidentifiable. If the professional knowledge exists, then the goals are set to fit the knowledge that such an IT terrorist can deliver. And the more accumulated knowledge is put in the game, the greater the threats.

- A crucial element and probably the main interim goal set by terrorists is [to] receive as much as possible media coverage for as long as possible. Generating publicity, propaganda campaigns and using the internet as a recruiting tool have proven to be very effective, which makes the internet even more attractive as a strategic target.

Why Do IT Experts Minimize the Threat?

The first reason is that they are guessing because they don't know the answer. It is not comprehendable that so many experts still hold the view that the terrorists don't have the knowledge, the professionalism and the means to cause deep and sustainable damage to our infrastructure. Tens of thousands of hacking events and network take-overs resulting in damages of billions of dollars happen every day, and the accumulated damage keeps mounting exponentially every year, in spite of better systems and better protection. We don't have yet any potent means to differentiate between challenge-hacking and terrorism-driven malicious-intended hacking. So how can the naysayers hold their ground? By pointing out that until now, there were no catastrophic results due to IT security breaching and attacks by hackers and/or terrorists. What they fail to tell, or prefer to forget, is that based on their own analysis, even results of several well-researched cyber attacks with no terror intentions, show that the immediate results and the fallout following the attack were disastrous. If so, what would be the result of a coordinated terrorist cyber attack?

Electronic Jihad

Jihadi websites become more and more "emancipated" and more upfront in defining the goals of their activity.... For example, [one website] has recently [redefined] the e-Jihad: "The electronic jihad is the method and the means to inflict maximum human, financial and morale damage on the enemy by using the internet." The website reiterates the importance of organizing synchronized mass attacks on anti-Islamic websites and calls on fellow Jihadists to sign up for the list of targets and to study the techniques and programs used in e-Jihad.

E-Jihadists are encouraged to believe that they are engaging in an online form of true Jihad, which isn't less important than physical Jihad, aspiring to become a shaiid (martyr). "The website distributes a program called Electronic Jihad that assists in overwhelming the servers of certain websites, thereby taking the websites offline, at least temporarily," writes Abdul Hammed Bakier in "Terrorism Focus."

Time and time again we see the typical arrogant approach so many security and IT experts take when analyzing terrorists' cyber attack capabilities. One can't but wonder if it isn't the same denying approach almost all experts have taken between the first attack on the Twin Towers [World Trade Center in New York City] in 1993 and the 9/11 attack. All signs and warnings were there but buying-in the collective dismissal of Al-Qeida's capability reminds me very much of the today's situation. . . .

Do Not Underestimate Cyberterrorists

We are bombarded daily by unsupported, sometimes doubtful evidence showing that the threat is not critical, reassuring us that terrorists are far from being able to launch a major dark-web cyber attack equivalent to the impact of 9/11. The following quote is one of hundreds like it: "Amid all the dire warnings and alarming statistics that the subject of cyberterrorism generates, it is important to remember one simple statistic: so far, there has been no recorded instance of a terrorist cyber attack in the US."

True, but not so evident as it may sound, because if one gathers the hundreds of cyber attempts and cyber attacks of what the naysayers define as "kid hacking," there is a growing volume of small damages that are painful to the attacked target which accumulates into a rather wider, deeper and more powerful disturbance of the networks and flow of information. And hasn't this exact phrase in various versions been chanted by renowned professionals and experts regarding Al-Qeida's capabilities until the very day of 9/11 when the first of the Twin Towers was hit? Haven't we been told then that Al-Qeida had limited potential; haven't we been reassured then that "we have taken all deemed necessary protective means to thwart such an attack?" We have been brain-washed by experts, the media and the academia, and most of us believed them.

Let's not repeat this dreadful mistake twice, let's not underestimate the enemy's capabilities, especially not those of the renewed, regenerated thriving Al-Qeida. Let's not decide in advance what their real capabilities are. We definitely know what their final goal is, the total reign of radical, fanatic Wahhabism [a conservative form of Islam] and total Jihad on Earth. And let us not forget that Jihadists are not rushing anything; they believe that time is in their favor.

"Terrorists prefer to inflict damage with physical means and then use the Internet to magnify the results of their handiwork."

Cyberterrorism Is Not a Serious Threat

Irving Lachow and Courtney Richardson

In the following viewpoint, Irving Lachow and Courtney Richardson argue that the threat of cyberterrorism is overstated. Terrorism, they maintain, is focused on the use of tactics that instill horror and fear, and Internet attacks do not create such fear. Rather than attacking the Internet, terrorists are using the network to communicate and propagandize, according to the authors. In any case, Lachow and Richardson contend, it would be difficult for terrorists to launch a successful cyberattack. Irving Lachow is senior research professor and Courtney Richardson is a research associate at National Defense University.

As you read, consider the following questions:

1. How does encryption technology help terrorists, in the view of the authors?

Irving Lachow and Courtney Richardson, "Terrorist Use of the Internet: The Real Story," *Joint Forces Quarterly*, 2007. Reproduced by permission.

2. According to Lachow and Richardson, how likely is it that terrorists are planning to launch a major cyberattack on the United States?

3. How many documented incidences of cyberterrorism against the United States have there been, according to the authors?

Cyberterrorism conjures images of infrastructure failures, economic disasters, and even large-scale loss of life. It also receives a great deal of coverage in the press. While the threat of cyberterrorism is real, the hype surrounding the issue often outpaces the magnitude of the threat. In addition, the term itself deflects attention from a more mundane but equally serious problem: terrorist organizations effectively using the Internet to stymie U.S. efforts to win the Long War [on terrorism].

The Internet enables terrorist groups to operate as either highly decentralized franchises or freelancers. Similar to information age businesses, these groups use the Internet to create a brand image, market themselves, recruit followers, raise capital, identify partners and suppliers, provide training materials, and even manage operations. As a result, these groups have become more numerous, agile, and well coordinated, all of which make them harder to stop. Furthermore, these groups have become expert at using the Internet to manipulate both public opinion and media coverage in ways that undermine American interests. In short, rather than attacking the Internet, terrorists are using it to survive and thrive.

This article examines why the Internet is so useful for terrorist organizations. It then considers how terrorists use the Internet for strategic advantage and why the threat of cyberterrorism may be overstated in many cases. . . .

How the Internet Helps Terrorists

The Internet has five characteristics that make it an ideal tool for terrorist organizations. First, it enables rapid communications. People can hold conversations in real time using instant messaging or Web forums. Instructions, intelligence information, and even funds can be sent and received in seconds via email.

Second, Internet use is a low-cost proposition. Terrorist organizations can now affordably duplicate many of the capabilities needed by modern militaries, governmental organizations, and businesses: a communications infrastructure, intelligence-gathering operation, training system, and media-savvy public affairs presence.

Third, the ubiquity of the Internet means that small terrorist groups can have a global cyber presence that rivals that of much larger organizations. Terrorists not only can communicate with each other from almost anywhere in the world, but they also can create a Web site that is viewed by millions and possibly even examined daily by media outlets for news stories.

Fourth, the growth in bandwidth combined with development of new software has enabled unsophisticated users to develop and disseminate complex information via the Internet. For example, in December 2004, "a militant Islamic chat room posted a 26-minute video clip with instructions on how to assemble a suicide bomb vest, along with a taped demonstration of its use on a model of a bus filled with passengers."

Finally, modern encryption technologies allow Internet users to surf the Web, transfer funds, and communicate anonymously—a serious (though not insurmountable) impediment to intelligence and law enforcement organizations trying to find, track, and catch terrorists. To achieve anonymity, terrorists can download various types of easy-to-use computer security software (some of which is commercial and some of which is freely available) or register for anonymous email accounts from providers such as Yahoo! or Hotmail.

Cyberterrorists Are Not Capable of Devastating Attacks

"Although cyberspace is constantly under attack from non-state actors, the attacks so far are generally not considered to be acts of terrorism," said [cybersecurity expert Dorothy] Denning. "There is some desire to conduct more damaging attacks, but there are no plans or capability to conduct devastating attacks against critical infrastructure or digital control systems," she said.

Breanne Wagner, National Defense Magazine, *July 2007.*

Using the Internet for Propaganda

The combination of characteristics described above makes the Internet a valued strategic asset for terrorists. In fact, one could argue that the Internet, along with other modern communications technologies, is a sine qua non of the modern global extremist movements. Successful terrorism requires the transformation of interested outsiders into dedicated insiders. Once someone has become an insider, less intense but still continuous interactions are required to maintain the needed level of commitment to the cause.

Before the advent of advanced communications technologies, this process was entirely based on face-to-face interactions, which limited the scope of a given group. However, the Internet allows groups to create and identify dedicated insiders—and to maintain fervor in those already dedicated to the cause—on a global scale. Advanced technologies also allow the extremists to deliver well-coordinated propaganda campaigns that increase the levels of support among the general public, which in turn allows terrorists to operate freely in these societies. For example, one of al Qaeda's goals is to use the Internet to create "resistance blockades" in order to prevent Western ideas from "further corrupting Islamic institutions, organizations, and ideas." One technique they use is to distribute Internet browsers that have been designed to filter out content from undesirable sources (for example, Western media) without the users' knowledge.

In summary, the development and proliferation of the Internet have enabled the rise of loose, decentralized networks of terrorists all working toward a common goal. In the words of one expert, "it is the strategic—not operational—objectives of the Jihadi movement's use of technology that engenders the most enduring and lethal threat to the United States over the long term."

Internet Attacks Do Not Create Enough Fear

It is evident that terrorist groups are extremely effective in using the Internet to further their missions. Are they also using, or planning to use, the Internet to launch a major cyber attack on the United States? We do not know, but there are a number of factors that suggest the answer to this question is no. Terrorism, by definition, is focused on obtaining desired political or social outcomes through the use of tactics that instill fear and horror in target populations. Cyberterror can be defined as:

> a computer-based attack or threat of attack intended to intimidate or coerce governments or societies in pursuit of goals that are political, religious, or ideological. The attack should be sufficiently destructive or disruptive to generate fear comparable to that from physical acts of terrorism. Attacks that lead to death or bodily injury, extended power outages, plane crashes, water contamination, or major economic losses would be examples. . . . Attacks that disrupt nonessential services or that are mainly a costly nuisance would not.

History shows that the vast majority of cyber attacks, even viruses that cause billions of dollars of damage to an economy, are not going to cause the levels of fear desired by most terrorists. In comparison, using physical means to create terror is fairly easy and quite effective. Put in these terms, it is not surprising that terrorists prefer to inflict damage with physical means and then use the Internet to magnify the results of their handiwork. Indeed, while there is clear evidence that terrorists have used the Internet to gather intelligence and coordinate efforts to launch physical attacks against various infrastructure targets, there has not been a single documented incidence of cyberterrorism against the U.S. Government.

Attacking Internet Difficult

One could argue that terrorists would use the Internet to attack cyber assets that control physical systems, thereby creating horrific physical effects via cyber means. The most likely scenario of this type is an attack on the control systems that manage parts of the Nation's infrastructure (for example, dams, trains, and powerplants). The consequences of an attack of this kind would be serious, so this threat deserves attention. However, the actual likelihood of such an attack is unknown; different analyses have reached different conclusions.

Two things are certain: successfully launching such an attack would not be easy, and the consequences are difficult to predict due to the incredible complexity and interdependence of critical infrastructures. Given a choice of conducting either a cyber attack whose consequences are unknown (and which may not have the desired effect even if it does work) or a physical attack that is almost certain to cause graphic deaths that will create fear, it is understandable why terrorists have (so far) chosen the latter.

> "Terrorist organizations such as al-Qaeda have studied biological weapons that can inflict the kind of indiscriminate mass casualties these groups seem to want."

Bioterrorism Is a Threat

Gerald Epstein

In the following viewpoint, Gerald Epstein argues that the risk of bioterrorism is increasing. Advances in biological technology, he claims, have provided terrorist groups with the capability to develop bioweapons. Epstein asserts that as the global workforce in the biological sciences increases, the likelihood that some workers will become terrorists grows as well. In addition, he contends, the dual-use nature of biology makes it difficult to take preventive measures against bioterrorists. Gerald Epstein is senior fellow for science and security at the U.S.-based Center for Strategic and International Studies, where he codirects the Biological Threat Reduction Project.

As you read, consider the following questions:

1. Why, in the author's view, is it more difficult to defend against bioterrorism than to commit a bioterrorist act?

Gerald Epstein "Bug Off," *Global Agenda*, 2006, pp. 184–85. Reproduced by permission of the author.

2. What are the "four Ds" that the author says should be used to frustrate bioterrorists?

3. How could our reaction to a biological attack help the terrorists achieve their aim, according to Epstein?

It is difficult to prove how serious the threat from bioterrorism is. True, several nations' bioweapons programmes demonstrated, long ago, that bacteria and viruses can kill over large areas and place many thousands of lives at risk. However, producing biological weapons agents and disseminating them effectively is not easy. It requires expertise, access to pathogens (from natural sources or laboratories), specialized equipment and experimentation. Bioweapons have rarely been used by terrorists, certainly not with the deadly effects of which these weapons are capable. So the bioterror threat has tended to play second-fiddle to the historically-established threat of epidemics and state-sponsored biological weapons programmes.

Unfortunately, technological and political trends all point towards an increased risk of bioterrorism. Continued advances in biological and other technologies have put much of the bioweapons capability that once required the resources of a state within the reach of non-state actors. Moreover, most of the necessary technology, materials and skills are "dual-use". They have legitimate applications in fighting disease, improving the quality of life, raising living standards and gaining a better understanding of the natural world and ourselves.

Inflicting Mass Murder

In the past, it was thought that terrorists' aim was exactly that: to inspire terror, usually by striking civilians unexpectedly, but in small numbers. Now, however, it is clear that a new type of terrorist seeks to inflict mass murder. We know that terrorist organizations such as al-Qaeda have studied biological weapons that can inflict the kind of indiscriminate mass casualties these groups seem to want. One might wonder why we have not yet suffered a major biological attack. Maybe not enough of today's terrorists have studied biology. Future terrorists may do so—and their biology classes will be more potent than today's.

Instead of debating whether terrorists who are comfortable with bombs, guns and suicide belts will succeed at mastering biology, we should recognize that, over time, the legitimate applications of biology and biotechnology will create an ever-growing global workforce that will already have mastered those skills. How confident can we be that none of these will sympathize with or become recruited by groups or individuals seeking to inflict widespread harm? Biologists becoming terrorists pose a greater challenge than terrorists becoming biologists.

Bioterrorism Presents Special Challenge

Bioterrorism, of course, is not the only source of biological risk. Traditionally, a key worry has been state biological weapons programmes. The Biological Weapons Convention, signed in 1972, banned the development, production and stock-piling of biological weapons (their use had been prohibited since 1925). However the American government reckons that several countries—including North Korea, Iran, Russia and China—maintain elements of an offensive biological weapons programme.

It is not only evil people who can wreak biological havoc. Naturally-occurring infectious diseases kill more than 13 million each year. The cumulative toll from AIDS exceeds 25 million, and there are worries that bird flu could kill on the scale of the 1918 flu epidemic, which claimed 50 million victims. Increasing global travel and growing population densities mean such diseases can spread more quickly than ever before.

Finally, more research and evaluation facilities—including, but not restricted to, those working on biodefence—are handling dangerous pathogens, so the chances of a pathogen escaping are increasing too. The mounting scientific and commercial applications of microorganisms increase the odds of their being used in ways that might have unforeseen adverse consequences.

Some measures that we are taking to counter, mitigate or respond to bioterrorism, such as improved disease-tracking efforts and preparations to address mass casualties, will also address these other threats. But there are some threats that need a more tailored response.

Even after getting policymakers' attention on the risks of bioterrorism vis-à-vis other biological threats, there are a host of other challenges in countering it. First, the pervasively dual-use nature of biotechnology means that measures designed to impede biological weapons development will also affect a wide range of legitimate activities. Moreover, scientific and technical advances—even (or especially) ones deriving from biodefence research—can expand the knowledge and skills base from which future weaponeers might draw.

Difficult to Defend

Traditional intelligence-gathering is not well suited to bioweapons-related activities. These have a very small "signature" and are difficult to distinguish from the vast, diverse and constantly-growing sea of legitimate biotechnology. Even if today's intelligence were perfect, it would not be good enough. Certain countermeasures will have long lead times, and so we must prepare today for threats well into the future.

Our problem is that it is simply much easier to attack than to defend. A defender must anticipate a vast range of conceivable attacks whereas the attacker need only select and accomplish one. Furthermore, defensive actions must be implemented within an extensive regulatory framework to ensure safety and efficacy. These strictures do not fetter

Biological Agents and Toxins

Threat	Mortality Rate (untreated)	Can Spread Person-To-Person
Bacteria		
Anthrax	high	no
Plague	high	yes
Tularemia	35%	no
Viruses		
Smallpox	30%	yes
Ebola	high	yes
Toxins (poisonous substances produced by living organisms)		
Botulinum	high	no
Ricin	high	no

TAKEN FROM: US Army.

attackers, who do not worry about legal compliance and who may not care about their own safety.

Given the diversity of potential biological attacks, any single response can address, at best, a part of the problem— and, given the complications above, incompletely at that. A concerted and coordinated web of actions will be needed to counter terrorist and national activities to develop, acquire and use effectively biological weapons. Traditional arms control, nonproliferation and military approaches still have a role, but they are increasingly unable to cope with changing technologies, threats and times. A new strategic approach is needed.

International Approach Is Necessary

The US-based Center for Strategic and International Studies is studying how biological threats can be reduced by taking an all-inclusive approach that is comprehensive, international and interdisciplinary.

We look at all stages of a possible bioweapons attack, aiming to frustrate them with "the four Ds": dissuading potential attackers and their unwitting accomplices by means such as codes of conduct for scientists and the criminalization of weapon-related activities; denying weapons programmes access to materials and expertise, for example, by tightening security at facilities housing dangerous pathogens; detecting illicit programmes, perhaps by alerting scientists to be sensitive to the possible misuse of biology; and defending against or managing the consequences of an attack, such as through improved epidemiological surveillance systems and development of broad-spectrum therapeutics (single products that can each counter a wide range of diseases).

Given our global transportation systems and interlinked economies, all of our fates are intertwined. A group based in one location can acquire resources in a second location to mount attacks in a third—attacks that can spread to many countries and that will have ramifications in many more. That is why we are developing an international programme through which we hope to give all nations a stake in biological threat reduction.

We are bringing a range of professions together to take concerted action against biological weapons threats. Traditional military and diplomatic approaches must be supplemented by new partnerships among the international scientific, public health, medical and law enforcement communities, local governments, private industry and others—communities that have different values, objectives, modes of behaviour and even languages. The deliberate use of disease for harm can simultaneously be a public health emergency, a crime, an act of aggression and the object of scientific investigation—and it will present each community that deals with these problems with a challenge that is familiar in some ways but novel in others. Countering such acts will require engagement and partnership.

We Must Not React with Fear

The arsenal of policy tools described above will raise barriers to bioweapons, portraying them as unattractive, difficult to develop covertly and unlikely to attain their users' desired consequences. However, we cannot achieve perfection. Therefore, we must react to biological attacks that may take place—in ways that do not create levels of social disruption that the initial act was unable to achieve. Our reaction must discourage, rather than encourage, attacks.

> *"The risk that terrorists will use biological agents is being systematically and deliberately exaggerated."*

The Threat of Bioterrorism Is Exaggerated

Milton Leitenberg

In the following viewpoint, Milton Leitenberg argues that the threat from bioterrorism has been exaggerated. According to the author, billions of dollars have been spent to combat bioterrorism without analyzing the risk or likelihood of a bioterrorist attack. The number of casualties from past bioterrorist attacks, he adds, shows that causing mass injuries and death with biological weapons is difficult. In fact, the publicity about bioterrorism concerns is what led terrorist groups to even consider them. Milton Leitenberg is a senior research scholar at the University of Maryland and the author of Assessing the Biological Weapons and Bioterrorism Threat.

As you read, consider the following questions:

1. What did former Senate majority leader Bill Frist say about the danger posed from bioterrorism, according to the author?

Milton Leitenberg "Bioterrorism, Hyped," *Los Angeles Times*, February 17, 2006. Reproduced by permission of the author.

2. How has the number of nations conducting offensive bioweapons programs changed over the past fifteen years, according to Leitenberg?

3. According to documents found by U.S. forces in Afghanistan, as cited by the author, how many pathogens for bioweapons had al Qaeda obtained?

The United States has spent at least $33 billion since 2002 to combat the threat of biological terrorism. The trouble is, the risk that terrorists will use biological agents is being systematically and deliberately exaggerated. And the U.S. government has been using most of its money to prepare for the wrong contingency.

A pandemic flu outbreak of the kind the world witnessed in 1918–19 could kill hundreds of millions of people. The only lethal biological attack in the United States—the anthrax mailings—killed five. But the annual budget for combating bioterror is more than $7 billion, while Congress passed [in 2006] a $3.8-billion emergency package to prepare for a flu outbreak.

Exaggerating the Threat

The exaggeration of the bioterror threat began more than a decade ago after the Japanese Aum Shinrikyo group released sarin gas in the Tokyo subways in 1995. The scaremongering has grown more acute since 9/11 and the mailing of anthrax-laced letters to Congress and media outlets in the fall of 2001. Now an edifice of institutes, programs and publicists with a vested interest in hyping the bioterror threat has grown, funded by the government and by foundations.

[In 2005], for example, Senate Majority Leader Bill Frist described bioterrorism as "the greatest existential threat we have in the world today." But how could he justify such a claim? Is bioterrorism a greater existential threat than global climate change, global poverty levels, wars and conflicts,

Funds Directed at Bioterrorism Could Be Better Spent

Like so many other instances when expert knowledge was discarded in the run-up to [the Iraq] war, the bioterror obsession could well have long-term consequences. "It has been four years of throwing money at a perceived threat with very little to show for it," says Columbia's Dr. [Irwin] Redlener. Many public health experts say that the billions spent preparing for these imagined threats have left the country dangerously unprepared for actual ones.

Jeremy Schill, Nation,
November 28, 2005.

nuclear proliferation, ocean-quality deterioration, deforestation, desertification, depletion of freshwater aquifers or the balancing of population growth and food production? Is it likely to kill more people than the more mundane scourges of AIDS, tuberculosis, malaria, measles and cholera, which kill more than 11 million people each year?

Threat Declining

So what substantiates the alarm and the massive federal spending on bioterrorism? There are two main sources of bioterrorism threats: first, from countries developing bioweapons, and second, from terrorist groups that might buy, steal or manufacture them.

The first threat is declining. U.S. intelligence estimates say the number of countries that conduct offensive bioweapons programs has fallen in the last 15 years from 13 to nine, as South Africa, Libya, Iraq and Cuba were dropped. There is no publicly available evidence that even the most hostile of the nine remaining countries—Syria and Iran—are ramping up their programs.

And, despite the fear that a hostile nation could help terrorists get biological weapons, no country has ever done so—even nations known to have trained terrorists.

It's more difficult to assess the risk of terrorists using bioweapons, especially because the perpetrators of the anthrax mailings have not been identified. If the perpetrators did not have access to assistance, materials or knowledge derived from the U.S. biodefense program, but had developed such sophistication independently, that would change our view of what a terrorist group might be capable of. So far, however, the history of terrorist experimentation with bioweapons has shown that killing large numbers of people isn't as easy as we've been led to believe.

Bioterrorism Has Few Successes

Followers of Bhagwan Shree Rajneesh succeeded in culturing and distributing salmonella in Oregon in 1984, sickening 751 people. Aum Shinrikyo failed in its attempts to obtain, produce and disperse anthrax and botulinum toxin between 1990 and 1994. Al Qaeda tried to develop bioweapons from 1997 until the U.S. invasion of Afghanistan in 2001, but declassified documents found by U.S. forces outside Kandahar indicate the group never obtained the necessary pathogens.

At a conference in Tokyo [in February 2006] bioterrorism experts called for new programs to counter the possibility that terrorists could genetically engineer new pathogens. Yet three of the leading scientists in the field have said there is no likelihood at this time that a terrorist group could perform such a feat.

The real problem is that a decade of widely broadcast discussion of what it takes to produce a bioweapon has provided terrorists with at least a rough roadmap. Until now, no terrorist group has had professionals with the skills to exploit the information—but the publicity may make it easier in the future.

There is no military or strategic justification for imputing to real-world terrorist groups capabilities that they do not possess. Yet no risk analysis was conducted before the $33 billion was spent.

Hype Promotes Terrorists' Interest

Some scientists and politicians privately acknowledge that the threat of bioterror attacks is exaggerated, but they argue that spending on bioterrorism prevention and response would be inadequate without it. But the persistent hype is not benign. It is almost certainly the single major factor in provoking interest in bioweapons among terrorist groups. [Osama] Bin Laden's deputy, the Egyptian doctor Ayman Zawahiri, wrote on a captured floppy disk that "we only became aware of (bioweapons) when the enemy drew our attention to them by repeatedly expressing concerns that they can be produced simply with easily available materials." We are creating our worst nightmare.

Periodical Bibliography

The following articles have been selected to supplement the diverse views presented in this chapter.

Daniel J. Barnett et al.   "Understanding Radiologic and Nuclear Terrorism as Public Health Threats: Preparedness and Response Perspectives," *Journal of Nuclear Medicine*, October 1, 2006.

Massimo Calabrezi   "The Other Nuke Nightmare," *Time*, February 14, 2005.

Thomas B. Cochran and Matthew G. McKinzie   "Detecting Nuclear Smuggling," *Scientific American*, April 2008.

Mimi Hall   "Experts to Testify of 'Real and Growing' Nuclear Threat to U.S.," *USA Today*, April 2, 2008.

Renee Montagne   "Colombia Reflects Rising Threat of Nuclear Terrorism," *NPR Morning Edition*, April 21, 2008. www.npr.org/templates/story/story.php?storyId=89803657.

Rocco Parascandola   "Stopping Attacks Like Times Square Blast May Be 'Almost Impossible,' Experts Say," *Newsday* March 6, 2008.

William C. Potter   "On Nuclear Terrorism," *Arms Control Today*, April 1, 2008.

Isabel Teotinio and Michelle Shephard   "Chilling Bomb Plot Alleged," *Toronto Star*, April 3, 2008.

Benjamin P. Thompson and Lawrence C. Bank   "Survey of Bioterrorism Risk in Buildings," *Journal of Architectual Engineering*, March 2008.

John Ullyot   "Nuclear Terrorism: Providing Medical Care and Meeting Basic Needs in the Aftermath," congressional testimony, May 15, 2008. http://hsgac.senate.gov.

CHAPTER 3

What Causes Terrorism?

Chapter Preface

Many claim that terrorism is caused by unjust conditions, such as poverty or lack of civil liberties, in various parts of the world and that eliminating these conditions would eliminate terrorism. Others, such as Middle East expert Daniel Pipes, say Islamic terrorists hope to establish a worldwide "caliphate," an Islamic government uniting all Muslim countries, founded on Sharia (a legal system based on Islamic principles of jurisprudence). It is likely that terrorism is caused by a combination of human rights issues and the desire of Muslim extremists to form a worldwide caliphate. While most people have a clear understanding of the human rights issues involved, many are confused by terms such as "caliphate," "Sunni," and "Shiite." Understanding these terms is important to determining the root causes of terrorism by Islamists.

The prophet Muhammad was both the founder of Islam and its political leader, combining both spiritual and temporal authority. The first pillar of Islam, the testimony of faith, is that "there is no God but God (Allah), and Muhammad is His Messenger." Submission and obedience to God were guided by revelations given to Muhammad, compiled in the Koran, and the example of Muhammad's own life. When Muhammad died, the community of Islam needed a successor. The word *caliph* is the English form of the Arabic word *khalifa*, short for *khalifatu rasulil-lah*, which means "successor to the messenger of God."

Disagreement over the selection of the first caliph is the source of the division between the Sunnis and Shiites in the Muslim world. Abu Bakr, the father of one of Muhammad's wives, was chosen as the first caliph. Sunnis believe that he and the next three caliphs rightfully took their place as leaders of Islam and that their successors, who ruled until the breakup of the Ottoman Empire after World War I, were legitimate.

Shiites, on the other hand, believe that Ali, the husband of Muhammad's only child, Fatima, should have succeeded Muhammad, and that the legitimate successors to Muhammad are Ali's heirs, whom they call imams. Although a Shiite caliphate arose under the Fatimids, the imams of the Ismailis who ruled in parts of North Africa from 908 to 1171, as well as in Egypt and Syria for part of this period, Sunni caliphates have mostly ruled in the Arab world.

In 1924, Turkish president Gazi Mustafa Kemal Ataturk abolished the caliphate and began westernizing Turkey. Other Muslim countries, such as Egypt, also began to secularize their governments and adopt Western systems of education and finance.

Four years later, in 1928, Hasan al-Banna founded the first Sunni fundamentalist movement, the Muslim Brotherhood, rejecting what he saw as the immorality of the westernization of the Islamic world. Today experts cite numerous examples of a renewed commitment to a worldwide caliphate. In 1998, Osama bin Laden predicted that "the pious caliphate will start from Afghanistan" and after the 9/11 attacks released a videotape calling the attacks "only a copy of what we have tasted. . . . Our Islamic nation has been tasting the same for more [than] eighty years of humiliation and disgrace, its sons killed and their blood spilled, its sanctities desecrated." In April 2008, Muslim cleric and Hamas member of the Palestinian parliament Yunis al-Astal stated on Al-Aqsa TV that militant Islam will accomplish "military conquests of the capitals of the entire world."

All Muslims do not agree that there should be a modern caliphate or what it would look like. However, as observed by the Center for Strategic Studies (CSS), "Muslims in the Middle East are exposed to the concept of the caliphate from a very young age, as it is part of history and therefore an integral part of one's education." Textbooks in the Middle East celebrate the bravery, justice, and egalitarian governance of the early caliphs. CSS notes that these teachings "lead people to see the classic caliphate period as the 'golden age' in Muslim history," and that the caliphate is often mentioned in speeches, debates, and at mosques. Although few Muslims advocate terrorism, nearly two-thirds of Egyptians, Indonesians, Pakistanis, and Moroccans surveyed in 2007 by World Public Opinion favored unifying all Islamic nations into a single Islamic state, or caliphate.

The authors of the following viewpoints debate the causes of modern terrorism.

> *"Terrorism is made a much more dangerous threat because poverty allows terrorists to manipulate people more easily."*

Poverty Promotes Terrorism

Andrew Whitehead

In the following viewpoint, Andrew Whitehead argues that poverty promotes terrorism. Terrorists, he maintains, exploit poverty to manipulate the poor and disenfranchised into serving the terrorist cause. According to Whitehead, terrorists can provide employment, enabling the poor to support their families. In addition, well-funded terrorist groups can provide social services and charity work that garners public support. Citing the experience of Egypt, the author claims that there is a clear correlation between terrorist violence and poverty. Andrew Whitehead is a policy analyst for the Homeland Security Policy Institute.

As you read, consider the following questions:

1. According to the author, what type of work do terrorists pay children in Iraq to do?
2. What social service project in Lebanon, cited by Whitehead, did Hizbollah fund that garnered public support for the group?

Andrew Whitehead, "Does Poverty Cause Terrorism?" Homeland Security Policy Institute, August 21, 2007. www.gwumc.edu/hspi. Reproduced by permission.

3. As described by the author, what did Egypt do that broke the link between poverty and terrorism?

Does poverty cause terrorism?

The short answer is: no. Rather than being a phenomenon of the world's poor, terrorism can just as easily arise among the wealthiest citizens of some of the world's wealthiest societies.

The long answer, however, is a little more complicated: poverty might not turn anyone into a terrorist, but it often makes the terrorists' goals easier to achieve.

If poverty caused terrorism, there probably would not be incidents like the botched attacks on London and Glasgow in June of [2007], attempted by what appears to be a terrorist ring of doctors and medical students. Osama bin Laden, himself a millionaire, is the son of a construction magnate with a fortune in the billions. His chief lieutenant in al-Qa'ida, Ayman al-Zawahiri, was a wealthy surgeon. Mohammed Atta, one of the 9/11 hijackers, completed a thesis in urban planning at a technical university in Germany. The list goes on.

Alan Krueger, an economist at Princeton University, has conducted a study of the economic backgrounds of terrorists around the world that backs up these anecdotes. "There is no evidence of a general tendency for impoverished or uneducated people to be more likely to support terrorism or join terrorist organizations than their higher-income, better-educated countrymen," he said at the London School of Economics. "As a group, terrorists are better educated and from wealthier families than the typical person in the same age group in the societies from which they originate."

Poverty Creates Opportunity for Terrorists

That is, there's little evidence that the deprivation and degradation of poverty—as awful as they are for billions of people around the world who live on less than $2 a day—are so en-

Poverty Is the Root of Terrorism

I believe terrorism cannot be won over by military action. Terrorism must be condemned in the strongest language. We must stand solidly against it, and find all the means to end it. We must address the root causes of terrorism to end it for all time to come. I believe that putting resources into improving the lives of the poor people is a better strategy than spending it on guns.

Muhammad Yunus,
Nobel Peace Prize speech, December 10, 2006.

raging that they cause people to adopt extremist ideologies, like that of al-Qa'ida. But poverty does create an opportunity for well-funded terrorists to manipulate people for their own ends.

The poor might be enticed to work for terrorist groups if they pay well enough or offer the only employment in town. In Iraq, thousands of children must work to support their families, and many are employed by insurgent groups. The children are paid to make explosives, clean weapons, transport bombs without attracting police attention, and a variety of other tasks. According to the UN Office for the Coordination of Humanitarian Affairs, these children earn a few dollars a day, often the only source of income for their families in a country where the unemployment rate is somewhere between 25 and 40 percent. It doesn't matter if the poor care about the terrorists' ideology or goals—if people are desperate enough, they'll make bombs anyway if it means a paycheck.

Poverty creates other opportunities for terrorist groups: poverty allows well-funded terrorists to garner public support by providing social services and performing charity work.

Terrorists Provide Social Services

Terrorists around the world spend hundreds of millions of dollars a year on these projects—including some of the most brutal, murderous, and tyrannical groups. Hamas, according to the Council on Foreign Relations, spends an estimated $70 million per year on schools, orphanages, mosques, healthcare clinics, soup kitchens, and sports leagues in the West Bank and Gaza Strip. Hizbollah funds, among other projects, Jihad al-Bina, or "Construction Jihad," dedicated to rebuilding houses destroyed in fighting with Israel. Terrorist groups from Colombia to Indonesia provide social services where government services are under-funded or nonexistent.

These groups wouldn't spend the money if it didn't produce results—increased popular support. Popular support can mean a lot of things to a terrorist group: supporters might provide recruits and hiding places, or simply not inform on terrorists hiding in their midst when the police come looking. It might also mean increased support for a terrorist group's political wing in elections. Hizbollah won all 23 parliamentary seats in southern Lebanon in 2005, while Hamas won 58% percent of parliamentary seats in the 2006 Palestinian elections. In situations where the terrorist group is competing for legitimacy with government, or seeks to overthrow it, popular support is a valuable tool in the terrorists' arsenal.

Terrorism and Poverty Linked in Egypt

This connection between poverty and terrorism was demonstrated in Egypt during the 1990s. One of the terrorist groups trying to overthrow the government, al-Gama'a al Islammiya (The Islamic Group), was composed primarily of poor Egyptians from the impoverished south of the country. Violence by the Islamic Group increased as poverty increased. Unemployment, rents, and farm foreclosures all rose rapidly in the first half of the 1990s. At the same time, deaths from terrorist violence rose from thirty in 1991 to 415 in 1995, increasing every year. When bread subsidies were cut and prices rose, so too did the rate of terrorist attacks.

The Egyptian government did not miss this connection. In 1996 it initiated a development program that poured tens of billions of dollars into the poor south of the country. Jobs were created, social services were expanded, and bread subsidies were reintroduced. The number of terrorist attacks began to drop every year until 1999, when the number of attacks reached zero and the Islamic Group declared a ceasefire. Meanwhile, other terrorist groups in Egypt, like al-Zawahiri's Islamic Jihad (made up of doctors and engineers from the wealthier north), refused to join the ceasefire and continued to plot attacks.

Of course, there were more factors at play than poverty. The members of the Islamic Group did not commit terrorism just because of poverty in their home villages, and they did not give up the fight simply because the government paid them off with development dollars. Terrorism is not a glorified bank robbery. But the Islamic Group was clearly able to tap into popular resentment over poverty in the south of Egypt to increase its ability to commit violence, and when economic conditions there improved, popular support for the group dropped off.

Poverty Helps Terrorists Flourish

Hamas and Hizbollah did not win their elections solely because of their charity work, and insurgents in Iraq do not recruit workers only because they can pay. But in each of these cases and more, terrorism is made a much more dangerous threat because poverty allows terrorists to manipulate people more easily. Though poverty does not cause terrorism, the U.S. and its allies must approach poverty around the world as one of the factors that helps terrorists flourish. Eliminating global poverty isn't just a humanitarian issue, but also an issue of national security.

❚ *"Terrorism is not caused by economic is-*
❚ *sues."*

Poverty Does Not Contribute to Terrorism

Daniel Mandel and Morton A. Klein

In the following viewpoint, Daniel Mandel and Morton A. Klein argue that terrorism is not caused by poverty. The authors point out that terrorists are often well-educated and affluent, with many having advanced degrees. It is not poverty and a lack of employment opportunities that cause people to become terrorists, they assert, it is ideology. The authors warn that raising living standards or providing economic aid to terrorist-sponsoring regimes will not solve the problem of terrorism. Morton A. Klein is national president of the Zionist Organization of America (ZOA) and Daniel Mandel directs the ZOA Center for Middle East Policy.

As you read, consider the following questions:

1. How many of the suspects arrested by British police in connection with the Glasgow airport terminal attack were health care professionals employed at British hospitals, according to the authors?

2. According to a report by Nasra Hassan cited by Mandel and Klein, how many of the 250 aspiring suicide-bombers in Palestine interviewed by Hassan were "un-educated, desperately poor, simple-minded or depressed"?

3. In the view of the authors, how has economic aid for terrorist-sponsoring regimes typically been used?

There is a common argument that terrorism is produced by poverty and suffering. If that is the case, the terrorists who attempted to crash vehicles into the Glasgow airport terminal in the United Kingdom [in July 2007] should have been poverty-stricken, underprivileged individuals. On the contrary, six of the eight suspects held by British police turned out to be young Muslim health care professionals employed at British hospitals. The common denominator was a hateful Islamist ideology, not poverty.

One suspect, Mohammed Asha, 26, is a neurosurgeon from Jordan who chose to live and work in Britain. Another one of the arrested bombers, Bilal Abdulla, qualified as a doctor in Baghdad before coming to Britain. A further suspect who was arrested in Brisbane, Australia, was a 27-year-old doctor who has been working as a registrar at an Australian hospital.

This is but one case among many that dispels the notion that Islamist terrorism is produced by poverty and hardship. The 9/11 hijackers were all educated Muslims, from affluent families, who subscribed to an extremist ideology of hate and murder. In fact, the Army Defense Intelligence Agency has disclosed that al Qaeda leaders whom they interrogated are often educated above a reasonable employment level and that a surprising number have graduate degrees and come from high-status families.

Terrorism Not Linked to Poverty

Several studies demonstrate no linkage between poverty and terrorism.

Terrorists Do Not Seek Prosperity

Terrorism is not caused by poverty. The terrorists of Sept. 11 did not attack America in order to make the Middle East richer. To the contrary, their stated goal was to repel any penetration of the prosperous culture of the industrialized "infidels" into their world.

The wealthy Osama bin Laden was not using his millions to build electric power plants or irrigation canals. If he and his terrorist minions wanted prosperity, they would seek to emulate the United States—not to destroy it.

Alex Epstein,
Israel Opinion, *September 10, 2006.*

A 2001 report by Nasra Hassan, a Pakistani relief worker, based on 250 interviews with Palestinian aspiring suicide-bombers and their recruiters concluded that "None were un-educated, desperately poor, simple-minded or depressed.... They all seemed to be entirely normal members of their families."

A poll the same year by the Palestinian Center for Policy and Survey Research indicated that Palestinians with more than 12 years' education were far more likely to support terror attacks than illiterate Palestinians.

A 2002 study by Princeton University economist Alan Krueger showed that members of the Lebanese terrorist group Hezbollah were less likely than other Lebanese to come from poor homes and more likely to have received a secondary school education.

A 2004 study by Dr. Marc Sageman, a psychiatrist at the University of Pennsylvania and a former CIA case office in Af-ghanistan during the late 1980s, concluded that "Most Arab terrorists . . . were well-educated, married men from middle- or upper-class families, in their mid-20s and psychologically stable."

To take one example among hundreds, Muhammad Abu Jamous, who was part of a terrorist squad that murdered four Israelis in Gaza on Jan. 9, 2002, was described by *The New York Times* as "a member of the Palestinian Navy [and] something of a minor celebrity. He had been a runner on the Palestinian national team, competing in Egypt and Saudi Arabia. He married just three months ago, and his wife is two months pregnant."

In other words, this terrorist had everything to lose—a good job, a wife and impending fatherhood. Yet, he picked up a gun and went out to murder innocent Israelis.

Economic Aid Is Not the Solution

The terrorist movement Hamas has murdered nearly 500 Israelis in seven years of suicide bombings and other attacks. Hamas makes clear in its Charter what motivates it: the goals of destroying Israel (Article 15) and the murder of Jews (Article 7), all based on Islamic texts.

Jews should be the least prone to the misconception that terrorism and violence is the product of economic causes. Across the centuries, those who attacked and murdered Jews— the Romans, Crusaders, Cossacks, Nazis—were driven by ideology, not poverty.

Understanding that terrorism is not caused by economic issues has immediate relevance. The United States and the world must not make policy on the false basis that a low standard of living is the problem and that economic aid for terrorist-sponsoring regimes like the Palestinian Authority is part of the solution. Such funding not only has failed to reduce terrorism in the past, but has often financed further terrorism.

Only reforming the Islamist media, mosques and schools that promote terror and hatred against the West, Christians and Jews can bring any hope of peace.

| *"Civil liberties are an important determinant of terrorism."*

Lack of Civil Liberties Causes Terrorism

Alan B. Krueger

In the following viewpoint, Alan B. Krueger argues that lack of civil liberties contributes to terrorism. Examining data on the country of origin of those who engage in terrorism, the author finds that most terrorists attack in their own countries, and that these countries tend to lack civil liberties. The same correlation holds true, he contends, for foreign insurgents in Iraq. Thus, according to Krueger, the United States should make regard for civil liberties an important element in its war on terrorism. Alan B. Krueger is Bendheim Professor of Economics and Public Affairs at Princeton University and the author of What Makes a Terrorist: Economics and the Roots of Terrorism, *from which the following selection is taken.*

As you read, consider the following questions:

1. What rights are associated with civil liberties, according to the author?

2. In Krueger's view, what is the effect of abridgment of civil liberties in the United States?

3. What concerns the author about the way the United States is attempting to build democracy in Iraq?

Interestingly, 88 percent of the time, terrorist attacks occur in the perpetrators' country of origin. This finding implies that most international terrorism is in fact *local*. Most of the terrorist attacks [are] carried out by residents of a country on property belonging to a foreign country, such as a McDonald's restaurant, or on foreign nationals who happened to be in the perpetrators' home country. Sometimes foreigners were the main target, and sometimes their deaths or injuries were strictly collateral. . . .

Lack of Liberty Spawns Terrorism

We also compared civil liberties among countries [where terrorism originates]. While some of the literature stresses the importance of political rights, in actuality civil liberties and political rights tend to be highly correlated. Political rights reflect the presence of democratic practices, such as open elections, while civil liberties reflect related rights, such as freedom of association and freedom of the press. It is difficult to distinguish between the two variables, although our data suggest that civil liberties may be slightly more important than political rights. We used data from the Freedom House Index, which rates countries based on civil liberties and political rights. The civil liberties indicator measures freedom of expression, freedom of assembly, and the presence of an independent judiciary.

Origin countries [for terrorism] tend to be countries with low levels of civil liberties. . . . Countries with low levels of civil liberties, such as Saudi Arabia, are more likely to be the countries of origin of the perpetrators of terrorist attacks. Countries with high levels of civil liberties are less likely to be origin countries. Within each of these groups of origin countries, countries with higher levels of civil liberties are slightly more likely to be targeted, although this is not an overwhelming effect. . . .

The [correlation between foreign insurgents in Iraq and] civil liberties were the same as in the international terrorism results: countries with fewer civil liberties were more likely to be source countries for foreign insurgents in Iraq. If we measured political rights instead of civil liberties, we found that foreign insurgents were coming from more totalitarian regimes. However, civil liberties were a more powerful predictor in these data. . . .

Civil Liberties Important in War on Terror

I believe that the importance of guaranteeing civil liberties has been underemphasized as a means of prosecuting the war on terrorism and the war in Iraq. The [George W.] Bush administration has emphasized the importance of building democracy, but civil liberties can be encouraged without occupying a country in order to impose democracy on it. I wrote an article for the *New York Times* in 2003 in which I argued that "a lack of civil liberties seems to be a main cause of terrorism around the world. Support for civil liberties should be part of the arsenal in the war against terrorism, both at home and abroad." [Former British prime minister] Tony Blair made a similar point when he said, "The more people live under democracy, with human liberty intact, the less inclined they or their states will be to indulge terrorism or to engage in it. This may be open to debate—though personally I agree with it—but it emphatically puts defeating the causes of terrorism alongside defeating the terrorist".

Protect Liberty at Home

I worry that the abridgment of civil liberties at home in the United States will be counterproductive. As Benjamin Franklin is credited with having written in his *Almanac*, "Those who

---

Repressive Regimes Promote Terrorism

Longstanding U.S. government support for repressive regimes—particularly in the Arab world, but in the Muslim world more broadly—has facilitated conditions where terrorism can emerge. . . .

Washington must, in both word and deed, make a clean break with its history of support for such regimes throughout the world.

U.S. Policy World, *October 2007.*

---

would give up Essential Liberty to purchase a little Temporary Safety, deserve neither Liberty nor Safety." Recall that Timothy McVeigh, who bombed the Alfred P. Murrah Federal Building in Oklahoma City on April 19, 1995, feared that the government had planted a microchip in him; he claimed he was responding to the government's actions at Waco and Ruby Ridge. The government's warrantless eavesdropping on American citizens and rampant misuse of "national security letters" to obtain confidential data are unlikely to reduce such paranoia.

Protect Liberty in Iraq

I also worry about the way in which the United States is attempting to build democracy in Iraq—sometimes by destroying civil liberties. A stated objective is to spread democracy to reduce terrorism, but it is not clear whether the main determinant of terrorism is democracy or civil liberties (which often go hand in hand with democracy). This desire for democracy above all else has resulted in the curtailment of civil liberties, such as the abuses in Guantánamo Bay and Abu Ghraib [U.S.-run prisoner of war camps]. Paul Bremer, when he was director of reconstruction and humanitarian assistance for the Coalition Provisional Authority in Iraq, closed down the newspaper *Al-Hawza* because of claims that it had incited violence. (It has since reopened.) Perhaps coincidentally, shortly after the newspaper was closed down, there were major protests and terror incidents. Additionally, the U.S. military has been paying a company called the Lincoln Group to plant stories in Iraqi newspapers, a strategy which seems counterproductive if one wants to build civil liberties.

Terrorism Is a Political Act

Neither the available micro-level data nor the more aggregated data show much of a correlation between income and the origins of terrorism. Likewise, educational attainment and involvement in terrorism, at both the individual level and the country level, are either uncorrelated or positively correlated. However, just as we often say that correlation is not proof of causality, lack of correlation does not necessarily imply lack of causality. This lack of correlation does, however, suggest to me that the burden of proof ought to shift to those who want to argue that low education, poverty, and other economic conditions are important causes of terrorism.

My research shows that civil liberties are an important determinant of terrorism. It is possible that there are some indirect links between economic conditions and civil liberties. Wealthier countries are more likely to protect their residents' civil liberties and political freedoms, so extremists in these countries might be less inclined to turn to terrorism to pursue their agendas. The data tell us that terrorism should be viewed more as a violent political act than as a response to economic conditions.

> "Violence . . . is at the core of [Islamic terrorist] beliefs that the infidel must be subordinated to Islam."

Islamic Fundamentalism Causes Terrorism

Zack Beauchamp

In the following viewpoint, Zack Beauchamp argues that Islamic fundamentalism is driving terrorism. Terrorist violence, he says, is not a response to U.S. foreign policy as some claim, but is theologically justified under terrorists' interpretation of Islam that Muslims should subjugate non-Muslims. The author contends that al Qaeda's goal is not merely to drive the West out of the Middle East but to establish a new caliphate that will create an Islamic world order. Zack Beauchamp writes for the Brown Daily Herald *in Providence, Rhode Island.*

As you read, consider the following questions:

1. According to the author, theological treatises by al Qaida members use what Arabic word to refer to the United States, Israel, and the West as a whole? What does that word mean?

2. According to writings of Osama bin Laden, quoted by Beauchamp, what is the relationship between Muslims and non-Muslims?

3. According to a former recruiter for Islamic fundamentalist groups cited by the author, how do Islamic fundamentalists react when people on television blame Western foreign policy for terrorism?

There's a tendency among many who, like me, identify on the left side of the political spectrum to treat terrorism as an issue with one fundamental cause: American foreign policy in the Middle East. According to this view, terrorist organizations are essentially resistance fighters against American imperialism and arrogance, reacting to everything from America's support of the Shah of Iran to its contemporary close ties with Israel.

It follows from this view that the obvious solution to the problem of terrorism is to leave the Middle East alone. If we close down military bases in Saudi Arabia, pull troops out of Iraq and cease preferential support of Israel, among other things, then the terrorists' motivation for violence will wane and eventually fade away. In Noam Chomsky's words: "Everyone's worried about stopping terrorism. Well, there's a really easy way: Stop participating in it."

Subordinate the Infidel

This view is fundamentally wrongheaded. It is impossible to deny that the invasion of Iraq and the lack of a real resolution to the Israeli-Palestinian conflict cause many in the Muslim world to sympathize with terrorist organizations (despite the fact that the latter is almost certainly not the fault of the United States.) However, American geopolitical maneuvering is not the primary motivation for the individuals who actually make up terrorist organizations. These terrorist organizations are committed to a fundamentalist interpretation of Islam that preaches violence not primarily as a response to American foreign policy, but because it is at the core of their beliefs that the infidel must be subordinated to Islam.

Some of the best evidence for this view comes from a recent article by Raymond Ibrahim, a scholar of Islamic history and culture who studied at Georgetown University's Center for Contemporary Arab Studies and is now a research librarian in the Near East section of the Library of Congress. Ibrahim found that in publicly accessible texts and videos (often with English translations and/or subtitles), Al Qaida's stated grievances fit quite neatly into the picture of the world painted by Chomsky and his ideological co-travelers. However, Ibrahim also found a wealth of untranslated works by al-Qaida members (including tracts by Osama bin Laden and Ayman al-Zawahiri) designed as theological treatises for both fundamentalists and the rest of the Muslim world. In these works—better indicators of Al Qaida's motivations than videos so tailored for Western audiences as to have English subtitles scrolling on the bottom—one almost never sees references to the United States, Israel, or even the West as a whole. Instead, they are subsumed under the Arabic word "kufr," or "infidelity," which Ibrahim translates as contextually meaning "the regrettable state of being non-Muslim that must always be fought through 'tongue and teeth.'"

Hate Shall Forever Reign

In these newly translated documents, there are places where bin Laden explicitly contradicts the propaganda he publishes for Western ears, and states that Islamic fundamentalists hate non-Muslims not because of their foreign policy decisions, but because they are not Muslims. In response to a letter published by a number of Saudi figures claiming that Muslims have a duty to respect non-Muslims and treat them kindly, bin Laden wrote, "As to the relationship between Muslims and infidels, this is summarized by the Most High's Word: 'We re-

nounce you. Enmity and hate shall forever reign between us—
'til you believe in Allah alone' ... 'Wage war against the infidels and hypocrites and be ruthless' ... Battle, animosity, and
hatred—directed from the Muslim to the infidel—is the foundation of our religion." In another work, bin Laden goes further: "The West is hostile to us on account of ... offensive jihad," a statement which flatly contradicts his propaganda's
claim that the West is assailing Islam and that al-Qaida is just
a resistance movement.

Laughing at the West

Bin Laden's newly translated texts are not the only support for
this view of Islamic fundamentalism. Hassan Butt, a former
recruiter for Islamic fundamentalist groups in Britain, cited by
Ibrahim, has stated that "when I was still a member of (a terrorist organization) ... I remember how we used to laugh in
celebration whenever people on TV proclaimed that the sole
cause for Islamic acts of terror ... was Western foreign policy.
By blaming the Government for our actions, those who pushed
this 'Blair's bombs' line did our propaganda work for us. More
important, they also helped to draw away any critical examination from the real engine of our violence: Islamic theology."

Fouad Hussein, a Jordanian journalist who had unprecedented access to Al Qaida's senior officials, found that the
organization's terminal goal is the establishment of a new caliphate [unified leadership of the Muslim world] designed not
merely to drive the West out of the Middle East, but to establish a "new world order."

Given this evidence, it is clear that Chomskyian isolation-
ism simply will not make terrorism go away. A truly effective
counterrorism policy must take into account the real motivations and beliefs of Islamic fundamentalists, and find a way to
ensure that their beliefs do not spread in the Muslim world.

Periodical Bibliography

The following articles have been selected to supplement the diverse views presented in this chapter.

Australian   "U.S. Brought Terror to Middle East: Ahmadinejad," March 4, 2008.

Tom Baldwin   "U.S. Admits That Iraq Is Terror 'Cause,'" *Times* (London), April 29, 2006.

Jeff Goodwin   "A Theory of Categorical Terrorism," *Social Forces*, June 1, 2006.

Chris Herlinger   "Nation in Peril," *Christian Century*, March 11, 2008.

Andrew C. McCarthy   "When Jihad Came to America," *Commentary*, March 2008.

Clark McCauley   "The Politics of Suicide Terrorism," *Middle East Journal*, October 1, 2005.

Laurie Mylroie   "A War on Terror Primer," *American Spectator*, March 2008.

Natalie O'Brien   "Latest Terrorists Are 'Looking for Thrills,'" *Australian*, March 10, 2008.

Justine A. Rosenthal   "Jigsaw Jihadism. (Controlling Religious Terrorism)," *National Interest*, January 1, 2007.

Roger Stahl   "In the Name of Terrorism," *Rhetoric & Public Affairs*, October 1, 2007.

Pat Twair and   "Bush's Marginalization of Mideast Historians
Samir Twair   Led to Iraq War Mistakes, Says Fawaz Gerges," *Washington Report on Middle East Affairs*, March 2008.

David Wessel   "Princeton Economist Says Lack of Civil Liberties, Not Poverty, Breeds Terrorism," *Wall Street Journal*, July 5, 2007.

OPPOSING
VIEWPOINTS®
SERIES

CHAPTER 4

How Should Governments Respond to Terrorism?

Chapter Preface

Former Israeli minister of defense Moshe Arens wrote in 2007 that "terrorists cannot be deterred. Their specific location is usually unknown, and punitive blows directed at the public that supports them tend to be counterproductive by creating additional support and sympathy for the terrorists throughout the world. Terrorists have to be fought." The United States has the largest military in the world. Terrorists are minuscule in number by comparison, and have no jet fighters, tanks, or battleships. Yet, terrorist groups manage to have a large impact on countries like the United States. Given this impact, countries must decide on the best method to fight terrorism—through warfare, rhetoric, or a combination of both.

U.S. National Security advisor Stephen Hadley, in a 2005 address to the Council on Foreign Relations, said that the short-term battle is one of arms. We must "use our military forces and other instruments of national power to fight the terrorists, deny them safe haven, and cut off their sources of support." But in the longer term we must win the battle of ideas. At the core of this battle, he said, is the need to encourage Islamic moderates to dispute the distorted vision of Islam advanced by the terrorists. "A struggle is under way for the soul of Islam—an ideological struggle for the support and loyalty of the Muslim world. Winning this struggle will require a direct challenge to the extremist voices within Islam," Hadley said.

The "battle of ideas" emphasizes theology as the singular defining attribute of Muslims. Amartya Sen, winner of the Nobel Prize in Economics in 1998, has observed that "an Islamist instigator of violence against infidels may want Muslims to forget that they have any identity other than being Islamic. What is surprising is that those who would like to quell that violence promote, in effect, the same intellectual disorientation by seeing Muslims primarily as members of an Islamic world." The world, he argues, is made "much more incendiary by the advocacy and popularity of single-dimensional categorization of human beings, which combines haziness of vision with increased scope for the exploitation of that haze by the champions of violence."

Aysha Chowdhry and Andrew Masloski, analysts with the Saban Center for Middle East Policy at the Brookings Institution, have written that the "battle of ideas" approach is counterproductive because it "encourages the concept of a Manichean struggle raging between two equally powerful and opposing world views, in effect legitimizing the extremists' understanding of the struggle." Chowdhry and Masloski claim that the policy also "overstates the extent to which [Osama] Bin Laden's world view constitutes a viable theological alternative for the world's 1.3 billion Muslims."

Chowdhry and Masloski propose an alternative to either the battle of arms or battle of ideas—cooperation with the Islamic world. According to these analysts, "Muslims share the same vision held by humanity everywhere—a secure future for their children and a life defined by dignity and liberty. Thus, policy makers should approach Muslims as partners on the path toward bettering livelihoods in Muslim societies." They argue that the United States needs to do three things: de-couple Islam and terrorism; recognize that most grievances expressed by extremists are secular and political in nature; and promote human dignity.

The authors in the following chapter present their views on effective responses to terrorism.

| *"Life-saving torture is not cruel. It is . . .*
| *morally justifiable."*

Torture Should Be Permitted to Fight Terrorism

Mirko Bagaric

In the following viewpoint, Mirko Bagaric argues that torture is morally justified in order to save lives of innocent people. Torture, he maintains, elicits reliable information that can prevent terrorist attacks. According to the author, closing the door on torture abdicates a potential means of preventing the killing of innocent people. Mirko Bagaric is author of Torture: When the Unthinkable Is Morally Permissable.

As you read, consider the following questions:

1. What medical analogy does the author cite to justify infliction of pain for a higher good?
2. According to a CIA agent cited by Bagaric, how quickly did an al Qaeda suspect begin answering questions after being subjected to "waterboarding"?
3. How does the author characterize persons who oppose torture in all circumstances?

Mirko Bagaric, "Some Torture a Needed Life-Saving Tool," *The Australian*, January 7, 2008. Reproduced by permission.

Just as the US administration is recovering from the stain of [the mistreatment of inmates at the Iraqi prisoner of war detention center] Abu Ghraib, it is now [January 2008] involved in another torture scandal. The US Government has announced that it is mounting a criminal investigation into the destruction of videotapes that depict the CIA allegedly torturing al-Qa'ida suspects.

No doubt this will lead to more fanatical claims by libertarian groups regarding the inappropriateness of torture. They are right that torture should never be used as a vehicle for punishment and domination. But different considerations follow when it is used for compassionate reasons: to save lives.

Killing Innocent People Worse than Torture

Paradoxically, people who propose an absolute ban on torture aren't sufficiently repulsed by torture and are too willing to accept the murder of innocent people: either they lack compassion or have a warped moral compass.

Torture is bad. Killing innocent people is worse. Some people are so depraved that they combine these evils and torture innocent people to death. Khalid Shaikh Mohammed, who is still gloating about personally beheading American journalist Daniel Pearl with his "blessed right hand", is just one exhibit.

Closing the door on torture involves abdicating a potential means of preventing the torture and killing of innocent people. Torture opponents need to take responsibility for the murder of innocent people if they reject torture when it is the only way to save innocent lives.

We must take responsibility not only for the things that we do but also for the things that we can, but fail, to prevent. Thus, it is morally repugnant to not throw a rope to a person drowning near a pier. That's why as a society we need to leave open the possibility of using torture where it is the only means available to prevent the murder of innocent people.

Torture Is Morally Justifiable

Life-saving torture is not cruel. It is motivated by a compassionate desire to avert moral catastrophes and it is morally justifiable because the right to life of innocent people trumps the physical integrity of wrongdoers.

Viewed in this way, torture has the same moral justification as other practices where we sacrifice the interests of one person for the greater good. A close analogy is life-saving organ and tissue transplants. Kidney and bone marrow transplants inflict high levels of pain and discomfort on donors. But the world is a better place for them because their pain is normally outweighed by the benefit to the recipient.

Such is the case with life-saving compassionate torture. The pain inflicted on the wrongdoer is manifestly outweighed by the benefit stemming from the lives saved. The fact that wrongdoers don't expressly consent to their mistreatment is irrelevant. Prisoners and enemy soldiers don't consent to the pain inflicted on them either, yet we're not about to empty our prisons or stop shooting enemy soldiers: this would be contrary to the common good.

Torture Elicits Reliable Information

There are four main reasons that have been advanced against torture. All are demonstrably unsound. First, it's claimed that torture doesn't elicit reliable information. This is factually wrong. There are countless counter-examples. Israeli authorities claim to have foiled 90 terrorist attacks by using coercive interrogation.

Retired CIA agent John Kiriakou has admitted to torturing al-Qa'ida suspect Abu Zubaydah, in a bid to obtain life-saving information. Kiriakou says the technique known as waterboarding broke Zubaydah in less than 35 seconds and that the suspect answered every question from that day on. The agent says he has no doubt that the information provided by Zubaydah "stopped terror attacks and saved lives".

Some Americans Support Using Torture

Do you think the use of torture against suspected terrorists in order to gain important information can often be justified, sometimes be justified, rarely be justified, or never be justified?

	Total Public
Often	15%
Sometimes	31%
Rarely	17%
Never	32%
Don't know/refused	5%

TAKEN FROM: Survey by Pew Research Center for the People & the Press, Oct. 12–24, 2005.

In more mundane situations, courts across the world have routinely thrown out confessions that are demonstrably true (because they are corroborated by objective evidence) on the basis that they were only made because the criminals were beaten up.

Slippery Slope Argument Is Defeatist

The second common objection to torture is that we can never be sure that the suspect has the relevant information. If that's the case, simply don't torture, in the same way that we're not permitted to shoot in self-defence until we're sure that the proposed target is up to no good.

It also contended that life-saving torture will lead down the slippery slope of other cruel practices. This is an intellectually defeatist argument. It tries to move the debate from what is on the table (life-saving torture) to situations where torture is used for reasons of domination and punishment, which is never justifiable.

A further common argument against torture is that it is inhumane and undemocratic. These are not reasons, just displays of venting. There could be nothing more inhumane than doing nothing as innocent people are being tortured to death.

Fanatical Opposition to Torture Is Extremism

Fanatics who oppose torture in all cases are adopting their own form of extremism. It is well-intentioned, but extremism in all its manifestations can lead to catastrophic consequences. Cruelty that is motivated by misguided kindness hurts no less.

In order for the anti-torture extremists to move from the base of the moral mountain, they need to accept that sometimes the only way to deal with evil is to hurt it and that evil is not transmittable.

In the end, we must always act in a manner that maximises net flourishing and inform our moral choices by reason, not reflexive emotion: that is the closest it comes to an absolute moral principle.

Kiriakou concedes that it was a tough call deciding that Abu Zubaydah should be tortured. But in the end he reasoned that he could not forgive himself if the CIA didn't use torture on a suspect and therefore didn't get "the nugget of information, and there was an attack".

If [other agents] refused to torture a suspect when it was apparent that it was the only means possible to save innocent lives, I don't think we could forgive them either.

> *"History does not give us one single example to support the claim that there can be such a thing as the responsible use of torture."*

Torture Is Never Justified

Brita Sydhoff

In the following viewpoint, Brita Sydhoff argues that torture can never be justified. The international prohibition against torture, she says, is absolute. According to Sydhoff, television shows justifying torture to fight terrorism attempt to shift our norms of right and wrong while dehumanizing the victims of torture. To permit torture is, in her view, to open a Pandora's box that will endanger us all. Brita Sydhoff is secretary-general of the International Rehabilitation Council for Torture Victims.

As you read, consider the following questions:

1. What example from the television show *24* does the author cite as misrepresenting the negative consequences of torture, and suggesting that torture is not as bad as it seems?
2. In addition to immediate pain, what else makes the effect of torture worse than its reputation in the view of Sydhoff?

3. According to the author, how many torturing governments have limited their use of torture to indisputable
ticking-bomb scenarios?

If the entertainment industry, not least Hollywood, reflects a
prevailing state of mind in the United States and the West
in general, torture may be steadily gaining acceptance as a
means of extracting information from suspects.

Or is it just a coincidence that the entertainment industry
increasingly appeals to its audience through scenes of torture
and violence at just the time when politicians and intellectuals
are arguing in favour of interrogation methods that amount
to torture, as a countermeasure in the so-called war on terror?

Hollywood Justifies Torture

In an earlier season of the popular Fox television series *24*,
Counter-Terrorist Unit (CTU) agent Jack Bauer fought a radical Islamist plot to cause meltdown at U.S. nuclear power
plants. The series is highly entertaining, but it is also a test of
its audience's views on the ticking bomb scenario: are they
prepared to condone torture if thousands of innocent lives are
at stake? Is it acceptable, for example, when a CTU agent
torture's his colleague's husband with electric cables in an attempt to extract the information that could possibly prevent
the meltdown?

The fact that *24* presents the enemies of the U.S. as dehu-
manized beings who are willing to kill even their own children in their terrorist fight against a democratic society sug-
gests that the upholders of law and life are left with no
alternatives. So that torture becomes acceptable in extreme
situations.

The series also gives the impression that torture is not always as bad as its reputation. In one scene, a CTU director
used a stun gun repeatedly against a female staff member who
was assumed to have knowledge that could prevent the melt-

down. What was her reaction when the director realized she was not involved in the plot? She was disappointed with her superior for mistrusting her, but then demanded a pay rise and went back to her desk. Just another bad day at work.

This presentation of what we can call the torture dilemma, combined with the minimization of the effects of torture, make it necessary to reiterate two facts that are increasingly questioned in anti-terrorist provisions:

Rule Against Torture Is Absolute

The prohibition against torture in international law is absolute: nothing can justify torture.

This principle is reflected in the United Nations Convention Against Torture amongst other international law instruments. The logic is that allowing torture in exceptional circumstances would open a Pandora's box and would lead to a situation in which states would be at liberty to respond to perceived extraordinary crises by diluting existing definitions of torture.

In the words of British international law expert Lord Hope of Craigshead: "A single instance [of torture], if approved to meet the threat of international terrorism, would establish a principle with the power to grow and expand so that everything that falls within it would be regarded as acceptable."

The U.S. detention camp at Guantanamo aptly illustrates the problem. The UN has criticized the U.S. for using interrogation methods amounting to torture against detainees at this camp. The U.S. government denies the charges, relying instead on its own interpretation of what constitutes torture, an interpretation that is far narrower than that of the UN convention, to which the U.S. is a signatory.

Torture Is Worse than Its Reputation

In the real world, torture is even worse than its reputation. Torture is not only about the immediate pain; it is also about the all-encompassing fear associated with being completely at the mercy of one's torturers.

Torture Is Barbarism

Torture is wrong because it inflicts unspeakable pain upon the body of a fellow human being who is entirely at our mercy. The tortured person is bound and helpless. The torturer stands over him with his instruments. There is no question of "unilateral disarmament," because the victim bears no arms, lacking even the use of the two arms he was born with. The inequality is total. To abuse or kill a person in such a circumstance is as radical a denial of common humanity as is possible.

Jonathan Schell,
Common Dreams, *January 20, 2005.*

In most cases, the actual physical and/or psychological abuse, coupled with complete helplessness, makes the victim's subsequent life a hell of depression, rage, anxiety, nightmares, and feelings of guilt, which are a few of the common consequences of torture. The victim's family is heavily affected, too. And all of this happens whether the victim is in fact "guilty" or not.

These two crucial factors—the slippery slope associated with questioning the absoluteness of the prohibition against torture, and the effects of torture in the real world—must be at the forefront of the debate at a time when leading democratic countries have implicitly or explicitly expressed reservations as to that absoluteness.

Torture Is Wrong No Matter Who Does It

Any attempt to open a Pandora's box—in entertainment or the real world—should raise deep concern. Torture is not something you walk away from with a disappointed shrug, whether at the hands of your boss at the office, hooded thugs in a soundproof room at the back of the local police station, or foreign soldiers in the dungeons of Abu Ghraib. And it is no less torture when secret agents working for democratic governments use stun guns or electric cables to interrogate another human being than when the henchmen of dictatorships pull their victims' fingernails or burn them with irons.

Those who claim otherwise are playing a dangerous game, and contributing to a treacherous discourse that has developed in the context of the war on terror—a discourse that has caused a slow but unmistakable shift of norms and values to suggest that torture can be used in a responsible and morally sound fashion. It cannot.

Torture Is a Slippery Slope

In empirical terms, history does not give us one single example to support the claim that there can be such a thing as the responsible use of torture. No torturing governments in the history of humanity, whether dictatorships or democracies, have limited their use of torture to indisputable ticking-bomb scenarios. If anything, the present U.S. government's policies on torture and the resulting abuses at detention facilities in Iraq and Afghanistan have confirmed the lesson that any opening, however small, that allows the use of torture will turn instantly into a festering gap, even when the perpetrator is a leading democracy.

The claim that there can be responsible use of torture ignores the fact that, even in theoretical terms, foolproof safeguards against mistakes (such as that of the stun gun incident in *24*) are not possible. Nothing can establish beyond doubt that the guy in custody is the right guy—that the information leading to his arrest is 100% reliable; that he has not been set up.

The logical next step is to allow torture on the grounds of "justified" suspicion. And so it goes. Accept a shift of norms, however small and well argued, and you blow the lid off Pandora's box.

Allow a little torture and no one will be entirely safe.

> "In view of the high priority that al-Qaeda accords to Iraq, the U.S. cannot discount Iraq's importance in the global struggle against terrorism."

Winning the Iraq War Will Decrease Terrorism

James Phillips

In the following viewpoint, James Phillips argues that winning the war in Iraq is vital to winning the war against terrorism. Al Qaeda, he says, has made Iraq a major front in its global terrorism campaign, shifting resources from Afghanistan for this purpose. The author claims that al Qaeda plans to establish an Islamic caliphate in Iraq, from which they will export jihad to other countries in the world. If the U.S. abandons Iraq, he concludes, the country will become a major source of terrorism for decades to come. James Phillips is a research fellow in Middle Eastern studies at the Heritage Foundation.

As you read, consider the following questions:

1. According to a letter from Osama bin Laden's chief lieutenant to al Qaeda in Iraq, which the author cites, where is the greatest battle of Islam currently taking place?

2. According to Phillips, what city was once the seat of the caliphate that al Qaeda seeks to reestablish?

3. As quoted by the author, what did General John Abizaid, the top commander of U.S. forces in the Middle East, warn would happen if U.S. forces left Iraq before finishing their mission?

Some who argue for an immediate pullout from Iraq call the war in Iraq a distraction from the broader war on terrorism. This argument ignores the fact that al-Qaeda has taken root in Iraq and massacres Iraqi civilians, government forces, and coalition forces on a daily basis. As President [George W.] Bush recently noted, Osama bin Laden recognizes the importance of Iraq, where, he proclaimed, the "third world war is raging." Abandoning the Iraqi government before it is able to provide for its own security would leave Iraq, its neighbors, and the United States more vulnerable to al-Qaeda and other terrorist groups. Whatever the disagreements over the relationship between al-Qaeda and Saddam Hussein's regime are, Iraq today is a strategically vital front in the war on terrorism.

Iraq a Major Terrorist Front

Al-Qaeda leaders have proclaimed Iraq a major front in their global terrorist campaign. This was made clear in a July 9, 2005, letter from Osama bin Laden's chief lieutenant, Ayman al-Zawahiri, to Abu Musab Zarqawi, who was then leader of al-Qaeda in Iraq. The letter was intercepted by coalition forces and subsequently published by the Office of the Director of National Intelligence, which expressed the "highest confidence" in its authenticity. In the letter, Zawahiri underscored the centrality of the war in Iraq for the global jihad:

> I want to be the first to congratulate you for what God has blessed you with in terms of fighting battle in the heart of the Islamic world, which was formerly the field for major

The Fate of Iraq Will Determine the War on Terror

The greatest threat Iraq's people face is terror, terror inflicted by extremists who value no life and who depend on the fear their wanton murder and destruction creates. They have poured acid into Iraq's dictatorial wounds and created many of their own.

Iraq is free and the terrorists cannot stand this. They hope to undermine our democratically elected government through the random killing of civilians. They want to destroy Iraq's future by assassinating our leading scientific, political and community leaders. Above all, they wish to spread fear.

Do not think that this is an Iraqi problem. This terrorist front is a threat to every free country in the world and their citizens. What is at stake is nothing less than our freedom and liberty. Confronting and dealing with this challenge is the responsibility of every liberal democracy that values its freedom. Iraq is the battle that will determine the war. If in continued partnership we have the strength of mind and commitment to defeat the terrorists and their ideology in Iraq, they will never be able to recover.

Nouri al-Maliki, address to Congress, July 26, 2006.

battles in Islam's history, and what is now the place for the greatest battle of Islam in this era. . . .

Zawahiri cautioned Zarqawi to avoid the mistake that the Taliban made in Afghanistan of alienating the Afghan people, who joined the opposition and cooperated with U.S. forces to overthrow the Taliban. He reminded Zarqawi that al-Qaeda needs some semblance of popular support to realize its plans for Iraq once American forces are driven out:

The first stage: Expel the Americans from Iraq.

The second stage: Establish an Islamic authority or amirate, then develop it and support it until it achieves the level of a caliphate—over as much territory as you can to spread its power in Iraq, i.e., in Sunni areas, is in order to fill the void stemming from the departure of the Americans, immediately upon their exit and before un-Islamic forces attempt to fill this void, whether those whom the Americans will leave behind them, or those among the un-Islamic forces who will try to jump at taking power.

There is no doubt that this amirate will enter into a fierce struggle with the foreign infidel forces, and those supporting them among the local forces, to put it in a state of constant preoccupation with defending itself, to make it impossible for it to establish a stable state which could proclaim a caliphate, and to keep the Jihadist groups in a constant state of war, until these forces find a chance to annihilate them.

The third stage: Extend the jihad wave to the secular countries neighboring Iraq.

The fourth stage: It may coincide with what came before: the clash with Israel, because Israel was established only to challenge any new Islamic entity.

Iraq as a Springboard for Terrorism

Al-Qaeda's strategy is clear. It seeks to carve out a state-within-a-state in Iraq to use as a springboard for exporting terrorism and subversion. Iraq looms much larger in al-Qaeda's plans than Afghanistan because of its strategic location in the heart of the Arab world; Iraq's close proximity to the Persian Gulf oil fields, a high-value target for attack; Iraq's usefulness as a staging area for attacks on neighboring countries and Israel; and the fact that Baghdad was once the seat of the caliphate that al-Qaeda seeks to recreate. As an Arab-dominated movement, al-Qaeda would have a much easier time operating from bases in Sunni Arab regions in Iraq than in Afghanistan or Pakistan, where Arab travelers stand out from the local population.

Bin Laden quickly grasped that Iraq was a more important front than Afghanistan in his global jihad and ordered many al-Qaeda forces to move there from Afghanistan in 2003. According to Taliban sources cited by *Newsweek*, bin Laden sent emissaries to meet with Taliban leaders in November 2003 to inform them that al-Qaeda was shifting resources and men from Afghanistan to Iraq.

In view of the high priority that al-Qaeda accords to Iraq, the U.S. cannot discount Iraq's importance in the global struggle against terrorism. Premature withdrawal from Iraq would demoralize the Iraqi government, tempt Iraqi officials to strike deals with insurgents or defect to the insurgency, and embolden al-Qaeda and other Islamic militants to escalate their terrorist campaign using Iraq as a sanctuary.

Terrorists Will Follow Us Home

The United States cannot afford to leave a power vacuum in Iraq. This would be a historic mistake, similar to the abandonment of Afghanistan after the Soviet withdrawal that allowed the Taliban to seize control and export terrorism around the world. The Bush Administration therefore is right to continue to help the Iraqis build a government that can defeat the insurgents and become an ally against terrorists, rather than a supporter of terrorism, as was Saddam's regime. If the U.S. abandons Iraq, it will become the next Afghanistan—a major source of terrorism, subversion, and warfare for decades to come. As General John Abizaid, the top commander of U.S. forces in the Middle East, recently warned, "If we leave, they will follow us."

> *"By energizing the jihadist groups, the Iraq conflict acted as a catalyst for the increasing globalization of the jihadist cause."*

The Iraq War Is Increasing Terrorism

Peter Bergen and Paul Cruickshank

In the following viewpoint, Peter Bergen and Paul Cruickshank argue that the war in Iraq has increased terrorism around the world. Suicide bombings in Iraq, they contend, have served as inspiration for similar bombings worldwide. The authors also claim that the Iraq war has reinforced al Qaeda's message that the United States is at war with Islam. As such, the war has energized jihadists across the world and increased popular contempt for the United States, all to the advantage of the Islamic militants. Peter Bergen and Paul Cruickshank are research fellows at the Center on Law and Security at the New York University School of Law.

As you read, consider the following questions:

1. According to the authors, by how much has the war in Iraq increased fatal jihadist attacks worldwide?

2. What effect has the war in Iraq had on Muslims' view of America, according to Bergen and Cruickshank?

3. According to the authors, how much money are insurgent and terrorist groups raising in Iraq from illegal activities?

"If we were not fighting and destroying this enemy in Iraq, they would not be idle. They would be plotting and killing Americans across the world and within our own borders. By fighting these terrorists in Iraq, Americans in uniform are defeating a direct threat to the American people." So said President [George W.] Bush on November 30, 2005, refining his earlier call to "bring them on." Jihadist terrorists, the administration's argument went, would be drawn to Iraq like moths to a flame, and would perish there rather than wreak havoc elsewhere in the world.

The president's argument conveyed two important assumptions: first, that the threat of jihadist terrorism to U.S. interests would have been greater without the war in Iraq, and second, that the war is reducing the overall global pool of terrorists. However, the White House has never cited any evidence for either of these assumptions, and none appears to be publicly available.

Iraq Creating New Generation of Terrorists

The administration's own National Intelligence Estimate on "Trends in Global Terrorism: Implications for the United States," circulated within the government in April 2006 and was partially declassified in October, states that "the Iraq War has become the 'cause celebre' for jihadists . . . and is shaping a new generation of terrorist leaders and operatives."

Yet administration officials have continued to suggest that there is no evidence any greater jihadist threat exists as a result of the Iraq War. "Are more terrorists being created in the world?" then-Secretary of Defense Donald Rumsfeld rhetorically asked during a press conference in September. "We don't know. The world doesn't know. There are not good metrics to determine how many people are being trained in a radical madrasa school in some country." In January 2007 Director of National Intelligence John Negroponte in congressional testimony stated that he was "not certain" that the Iraq War had been a recruiting tool for Al Qaeda and played down the likely impact of the war on jihadists worldwide: "I wouldn't say there has been a widespread growth in Islamic extremism beyond Iraq. I really wouldn't."

Indeed, though what we will call "The Iraq Effect" is a crucial matter for U.S. national security, we have found no statistical documentation of its existence and gravity, at least in the public domain. In this report, we have undertaken what we believe to be the first such study, using information from the world's premier database on global terrorism. The results are being published for the first time by *Mother Jones*, the news and investigative magazine, as part of a broader "Iraq 101" package in the magazine's March/April 2007 issue.

Terror Attacks Increased Sevenfold

Our study shows that the Iraq War has generated a stunning sevenfold increase in the yearly rate of fatal jihadist attacks, amounting to literally hundreds of additional terrorist attacks and thousands of civilian lives lost; even when terrorism in Iraq and Afghanistan is excluded, fatal attacks in the rest of the world have increased by more than one-third.

We are not making the argument that without the Iraq War, jihadist terrorism would not exist, but our study shows that the Iraq conflict has greatly increased the spread of the Al Qaeda ideological virus, as shown by a rising number of terrorist attacks in the past three years [2004–2007] from London to Kabul, and from Madrid to the Red Sea. . . .

Our study yields one resounding finding: The rate of terrorist attacks around the world by jihadist groups and the rate of fatalities in those attacks increased dramatically after the invasion of Iraq. Globally there was a 607 percent rise in the average yearly incidence of attacks (28.3 attacks per year before and 199.8 after) and a 237 percent rise in the average fatality rate (from 501 to 1,689 deaths per year). A large part of this rise occurred in Iraq, which accounts for fully half of the global total of jihadist terrorist attacks in the post–Iraq War period. But even excluding Iraq, the average yearly number of jihadist terrorist attacks and resulting fatalities still rose sharply around the world by 265 percent and 58 percent respectively.

And even when attacks in both Afghanistan and Iraq (the two countries that together account for 80 percent of attacks and 67 percent of deaths since the invasion of Iraq) are excluded, there has still been a significant rise in jihadist terrorism elsewhere—a 35 percent increase in the number of jihadist terrorist attacks outside of Afghanistan and Iraq, from 27.6 to 37 a year, with a 12 percent rise in fatalities from 496 to 554 per year.

Of course, just because jihadist terrorism has risen in the period after the invasion of Iraq, it does not follow that events in Iraq itself caused the change. For example, a rise in attacks in the Kashmir conflict and the Chechen separatist war against Russian forces may have nothing to do with the war in Iraq. But the most direct test of The Iraq Effect—whether the United States and its allies have suffered more jihadist terrorism after the invasion than before—shows that the rate of jihadist attacks on Western interests and citizens around the world (outside of Afghanistan and Iraq) has risen by a quarter, from 7.2 to 9 a year, while the yearly fatality rate in these attacks has increased by 4 percent from 191 to 198.

Some Positive Findings

One of the few positive findings of our study is that only 18 American civilians (not counting civilian contractors in Iraq and Afghanistan) have been killed by jihadist groups since the war in Iraq began. But that number is still significantly higher than the four American civilians who were killed in attacks attributed to jihadist groups in the period between 9/11 and the Iraq War. It was the capture and killing of much of Al Qaeda's leadership after 9/11 and the breakup of its training camp facilities in Afghanistan—not the war in Iraq—that prevented Al Qaeda from successfully launching attacks on American targets on the scale it did in the years before 9/11.

Also undermining the argument that Al Qaeda and like-minded groups are being distracted from plotting against Western targets are the dangerous, anti-American plots that have arisen since the start of the Iraq War. Jihadist terrorists have attacked key American allies since the Iraq conflict began, mounting multiple bombings in London that killed 52 in July 2005, and attacks in Madrid in 2004 that killed 191. Shehzad Tanweer, one of the London bombers, stated in his videotaped suicide "will," "What have you witnessed now is only the beginning of a string of attacks that will continue and become stronger until you pull your forces out of Afghanistan and Iraq." There have been six jihadist attacks on the home soil of the United States' NATO [North Atlantic Treaty Organization] allies (including Turkey) in the period after the invasion of Iraq, whereas there were none in the 18 months following 9/11; and, of course, the plan uncovered in London in August 2006 to smuggle liquid explosives onto U.S. airliners, had it succeeded, would have killed thousands.

Al-Qaeda Still Focused on America

Al Qaeda has not let the Iraq War distract it from targeting the United States and her allies. In a January 19, 2006 audiotape, Osama bin Laden himself refuted President Bush's argument that Iraq had distracted and diverted Al Qaeda: "The reality shows that that the war against America and its allies has not remained limited to Iraq, as he [President Bush] claims, but rather, that Iraq has become a source and attraction and recruitment of qualified people. . . . As for the delay in similar [terrorist] operations in America, [the] operations are being prepared, and you will witness them, in your own land, as soon as preparations are complete."

Ayman al Zawahiri echoed bin Laden's words in a March 4, 2006, videotape broadcast by Al Jazeera calling for jihadists to launch attacks on the home soil of Western countries: "[Muslims have to] inflict losses on the crusader West, especially to its economic infrastructure with strikes that would make it bleed for years. The strikes on New York, Washington, Madrid, and London are the best examples."

Popular Contempt for U.S. Policy

One measure of the impact of the Iraq War is the precipitous drop in public support for the United States in Muslim countries. Jordan, a key U.S. ally, saw popular approval for the United States drop from 25 percent in 2002 to 1 percent in 2003. In Lebanon during the same period, favorable views of the United States dropped from 30 percent to 15 percent, and in the world's largest Muslim country, Indonesia, favorable views plummeted from 61 percent to 15 percent. Disliking the United States does not make you a terrorist, but clearly the pool of Muslims who dislike the United States has grown by hundreds of millions since the Iraq War began. The United States' plummeting popularity does not suggest active popular support for jihadist terrorists but it does imply some sympathy with their anti-American posture, which means a significant swath of the Muslim population cannot be relied on as an effective party in counter-terrorism/insurgency measures. And so, popular contempt for U.S. policy has become a force multiplier for Islamist militants.

The Iraq War has also encouraged Muslim youth around the world to join jihadist groups, not necessarily directly tied to Al Qaeda but often motivated by a similar ideology. The Iraq War allowed Al Qaeda, which was on the ropes in 2002

Iraq War Gives Terrorists What They Want

President [George W. Bush] would have us believe that every bomb in Baghdad is part of al Qaeda's war against us, not an Iraqi civil war. He elevates al Qaeda in Iraq—which didn't exist before our invasion—and overlooks the people who hit us on 9/11, who are training new recruits in Pakistan. He lumps together groups with very different goals: al Qaeda and Iran, Shiite militias and Sunni insurgents. He confuses our mission.

And worse—he is fighting the war the terrorists want us to fight. [Osama] Bin Ladin and his allies know they cannot defeat us on the field of battle or in a genuine battle of ideas. But they can provoke the reaction we've seen in Iraq: a misguided invasion of a Muslim country that sparks new insurgencies, ties down our military, busts our budgets, increases the pool of terrorist recruits, alienates America, gives democracy a bad name, and prompts the American people to question our engagement in the world.

By refusing to end the war in Iraq, President Bush is giving the terrorists what they really want, and what the Congress voted to give them in 2002: a U.S. occupation of undetermined length, at undetermined cost, with undetermined consequences.

Barack Obama,
"The War We Need to Win," August 1, 2007.

after the United States had captured or killed two-thirds of its leadership, to reinvent itself as a broader movement because Al Qaeda's central message—that the United States is at war with Islam—was judged by significant numbers of Muslims to have been corroborated by the war in Iraq. And compounding this, the wide dissemination of the exploits of jihadist groups in Iraq following the invasion energized potential and actual jihadists across the world. . . .

Iraq War Promoting Terrorism Worldwide

Our survey shows that the Iraq conflict has motivated jihadists around the world to see their particular struggle as part of a wider global jihad fought on behalf of the Islamic ummah, the global community of Muslim believers. The Iraq War had a strong impact in jihadist circles in the Arab world and Europe, but also on the Taliban, which previously had been quite insulated from events elsewhere in the Muslim world. By energizing the jihadist groups, the Iraq conflict acted as a catalyst for the increasing globalization of the jihadist cause, a trend that should be deeply troubling for American policymakers. In the late 1990s, bin Laden pushed a message of a global jihad and attracted recruits from around the Muslim world to train and fight in Afghanistan. The Iraq War has made bin Laden's message of global struggle even more persuasive to militants. Over the past three years, Iraq has attracted thousands of foreign fighters who have been responsible for the majority of suicide attacks in the country. Those attacks have had an enormous strategic impact; for instance, getting the United Nations to pull out of Iraq and sparking the Iraqi civil war. . . .

Already terrorist groups in Iraq may be in a position to start sending funds to other jihadist fronts. According to a U.S. government report leaked to the *New York Times* in November 2006, the fact that insurgent and terrorist groups are raising up to $200 million a year from various illegal activities such as kidnapping and oil theft in Iraq means that they "may have surplus funds with which to support other terrorist organizations outside Iraq." Indeed, a letter from Al Qaeda's No. 2, Ayman al Zawahiri, to Al Qaeda in Iraq leader Abu Musab al Zarqawi in July 2005 contained this revealing request: "Many of the [funding] lines have been cut off. Because of this we need a payment while new lines are being opened. So if you're capable of sending a payment of approximately one hundred thousand we'll be very grateful to you."

The "globalization of martyrdom" prompted by the Iraq War has not only attracted foreign fighters to die in Iraq (we record 148 suicide-terrorist attacks in Iraq credited to an identified jihadist group) but has also encouraged jihadists to conduct many more suicide operations elsewhere. Since the U.S. invasion of Iraq, there has been a 246 percent rise in the rate of suicide attacks (6 before and 47 after) by jihadist groups outside of Iraq and a 24 percent increase in the corresponding fatality rate. Even excluding Afghanistan, there has been a 150 percent rise in the rate of suicide attacks and a 14 percent increase in the rate of fatalities attributable to jihadists worldwide. The reasons for the spread of suicide bombing attacks in other jihadist theaters are complex but the success of these tactics in Iraq, the lionization that Iraqi martyrs receive on jihadist websites, and the increase in feelings of anger and frustration caused by images of the Iraq War have all likely contributed significantly. The spread of suicide bombings should be of great concern to the United States in defending its interests and citizens around the world, because they are virtually impossible to defend against.

Hardline Jihad

The Iraq War has also encouraged the spread of more hardline forms of jihad (the corollary to an increase in suicide bombing). Anger and frustration over Iraq has increased the popularity, especially among young militants, of a hardcore takfiri ideology that is deeply intolerant of divergent interpretations of Islam and highly tolerant of extreme forms of violence. The visceral anti-Americanism, anti-Semitism, and anti-Shiism widely circulated among the Internet circles around ideologues such as Abu Muhammad al-Maqdisi and Abu Qatada (both Jordanian-Palestinian mentors to Abu Musab al

Zarqawi) and Al Qaeda's Syrian hawk, Mustafa Setmariam Nasar, are even more extreme, unlikely as it may sound, than the statements of bin Laden himself.

Our study shows just how counterproductive the Iraq War has been to the war on terrorism. The most recent State Department report on global terrorism states that the goal of the United States is to identify, target, and prevent the spread of "jihadist groups focused on attacking the United States or its allies [and those groups that] view governments and leaders in the Muslim world as their primary targets." Yet, since the invasion of Iraq, attacks by such groups have risen more than sevenfold around the world. And though few Americans have been killed by jihadist terrorists in the past three years, it is wishful thinking to believe that this will continue to be the case, given the continued determination of militant jihadists to target the country they see as their main enemy. We will be living with the consequences of the Iraq debacle for more than a decade.

> "If our goal is to roll back terrorism and reduce its global appeal, sooner or later we are going to have to deal directly with terrorists."

Governments Should Negotiate with Terrorists

Douglas A. Borer

In the following viewpoint, Douglas A. Borer argues that negotiating with terrorists is inevitable if we want to win the war on terrorism. While killing Osama bin Laden may be good revenge for 9/11, he says, bin Laden's death will not cause terrorists to give up. Borer adds that negotiations do not mean that we give up other options, such as armed conflict. Even if negotiations fail, he argues, the attempt cannot harm us and could undermine bin Laden's legitimacy in the Muslim world. Douglas A. Borer is author of Superpowers Defeated: Vietnam and Afghanistan Compared.

As you read, consider the following questions:

1. What U.S. president does the author say successfully negotiated with the leading state-sponsor of terror in modern times?

Douglas A. Borer, "Why Not Test Bin Laden's 'Truce' Offer?" *The Christian Science Monitor*, January 24, 2006. www.csmonitor.com. Reproduced by permission.

2. With what terrorist groups did Indonesia and Britain successfully negoitate peace, according to Borer?

3. How did failed negotiations between Colombia and FARC terrorists, according to the author, nonetheless produce a positive result?

One of the hardest decisions a president of the United States is obligated to make is that of going to war. It is a decision, however, that pales in comparison to the degree of difficulty in making peace when one's enemy remains unvanquished. With the release of Osama bin Laden's latest [January 2006] media communiqué offering a truce to the US, President [George W.] Bush must decide whether to stick to the moribund old cliché "we don't negotiate with terrorists," or whether he should use this as a potential opportunity to redirect global politics along a path that serves US national interests.

Everyone Negotiates with Terrorists

Truth be told, almost all nation-states, including our own, have negotiated with terrorists. Israel's tough old soldier Yitzhak Rabin buried the hatchet with Yasser Arafat, and thus engendered a peace process that, despite many fits and starts, has steadily moved toward the creation of an independent and democratic Palestinian state. A vocal minority called Rabin soft on terrorism, but most Israelis understood he was acting in the country's best interests. President [Ronald] Reagan was credited for negotiating the release of American hostages with Iran, the leading state-sponsor of terror in modern times.

Under Reagan and the first President Bush, Iraq was removed from the State Department's list of terror sponsors in order to enable diplomatic engagement. When diplomacy failed and Saddam Hussein invaded Kuwait, Mr. Bush adroitly marshaled the finest international coalition ever to be assembled. He lost the next US presidential election, but not because of his policies toward Iraq. Recently, Indonesia and Britain have made peace with Aceh [the Free Aceh Movement] and IRA [Irish Republican Army] terrorists respectively, and the US has come to terms with Libya's terrorist-sponsoring leader Muammar Qaddafi. Despite the tired public rhetoric of denial, negotiating with terrorists is the norm in international affairs.

Reduce Terrorism Through Negotiation

Regrettably, even though we continue to eliminate Al Qaeda operatives in Pakistan and other locales, due in part to the collateral damage these strikes produce, there seems to be no shortage of enraged Muslims to take their place. Indeed, the US invasion of Iraq has been judged by many experts as the premier recruiting tool for the global jihadist movement. Simply put, there are more anti-US Muslims willing to use terror to strike at us today than there were on Sept. 11, 2001.

If our goal is to reverse this trend, the question is simple: Are we better off negotiating with Mr. bin Laden? If we can capture or kill him, certainly the US can rightfully claim justice has been served against the perpetrators of 9/11. Because revenge is the sweetest of our dark sweet dreams, bin Laden's demise will bring no small degree of personal satisfaction to many people. But if we kill him with a well-aimed smart bomb, or if he remains in hiding as a living symbol of a growing anti-US resistance in the Muslim world, will the insurgents in Iraq and Afghanistan lay down their arms? Leading US government officials have said time and again that bin Laden's death or capture will not engender these results. Thus, if our wisest men have decided that our present policy toward bin Laden will not help reduce the threat of terrorism, what might help? Does our yearning for revenge outweigh the potential value we might gain by negotiating with bin Laden?

Negotiation Cannot Hurt

If our goal is to roll back terrorism and reduce its global appeal, sooner or later we are going to have to deal directly with terrorists. Even if such negotiations fail, history has shown that a silver lining is often found. In Colombia, the [Andrés] Pastrana administration pursued peace with FARC [Revolutionary Armed Forces of Colombia People's Army] terrorists only to find that they were false partners. FARC's duplicity revealed to the Colombian people that a military response was necessary, and this energized the Colombian government to legitimately escalate the war.

> *"Despite the compelling reasons to negotiate [with terrorists], the policy of non-negotiation has been practiced for many sound reasons that hold true today like they always have."*

Governments Should Not Negotiate with Terrorists

Mike Wacker

In the following viewpoint, Mike Wacker argues that refusing to negotiate with terrorists is a sound policy. Terrorists, he asserts, do not keep their word, and negotiating with terrorists in some cases, such as for release of hostages, encourages more terrorism by rewarding the perpetrators with cash, weapons, or the release of fellow-prisoners. Negotiating with terrorists, he concludes, can actually encourage the spread of terrorism. Mike Wacker is a blogger and assistant Web editor at the Cornell Daily Sun.

As you read, consider the following questions:

1. What proves, according to the author, that terrorists are irrational and unreliable negotiating partners?

2. Why does Afghanistan refuse to exchange Taliban prisoners for hostages, according to Wacker?

Mike Wacker, "Negotiating with the Wrong People," *The Cornell Daily Sun*, August 2, 2007. http://cornellsun.com. Reproduced by permission.

3. In the author's view, how will those who oppose the United States or its allies react to any weaknesses they may sense?

While many nations including the United States have long refused to negotiate with terrorists, the latest [August 2007] hostage crisis in Afghanistan has renewed the debate over the policy of non-negotiation. Not only did the Taliban kidnap 23 innocent Christian missionaries from South Korea, demanding an exchange for Taliban prisoners, but they have also killed some of the hostages already, ratcheting up the pressure to cut a deal to save the rest. Even if South Korea and the Afghan government find a way to buy more time for the hostages, it may not help the seriously ill hostages who face the prospect of death merely by remaining in captivity. Despite the compelling reasons to negotiate in this scenario, however, the policy of non-negotiation has been practiced for many sound reasons that hold true today like they always have.

Terrorists Are Not Trustworthy

First of all, terrorists are not exactly trustworthy. They do not always honor their deals. This takes place not only when they flagrantly refuse to hold up their own end of the deal, but also when they creatively reinterpret any deal to their favor. Based on how Islamic extremists reinterpret the Quran, one could easily see them reinterpreting a lot with their perverted worldview. In these negotiations, the other side is not a civilized leader of a respectable democratic nation. It's not even an Iranian leader who despite his craziness has to worry about both the effect of sanctions on his nation as well as the many Iranians who have cooled to his hard-line views. The other side engages in terrorism! They do not think rationally. In the case of the Korean hostages, there is even a precedent for this irrational behavior noted by *The Times*; the Taliban has already broken a truce which should have lasted until Wednesday at noon,

Terrorists Are Insincere Negotiators

Too often Western powers try to make negotiating partners out of dictators and terrorists. Seldom does this curb terrorism. Prior to the September 11, 2001 terrorist attacks, senior State Department official Robin Rafael, for example, counseled the U.S. government to accommodate the Taliban. Diplomatic promises are as ephemeral as terrorists' sincerity. The Taliban embraced engagement to entrench. The Palestinian Authority embraced engagement to rearm. Meanwhile, the Taliban's regime facilitated al-Qaeda and Palestinian Authority leader Yasir Arafat equipped his proxy militias with far more lethal weapons, explosives, and missiles.

Michael Rubin and Suzanne Gershowitz,
Middle East Forum, *July 12, 2006.*

prematurely killing one of the hostages. Given all of this, it cannot possibly be rational at all to deal with such irrational people.

Negotiation Encourages More Terrorism

While negotiating for the release of hostages may pay off in the short term, in the longer term this strategy will always backfire. For one, the chance of more abductions and hostage-taking increases. The idea is quite simple; if the terrorists can get cash, weapons, prisoners releases, or anything in exchange for a nation's hostages, they will be more inclined to take hostages again. Why take hostages from a nation that strongly refuses to negotiate with terrorists when the terrorists can instead choose a nation who will willingly and openly negotiate? Furthermore, any nation or group that gives the terrorists anything at all in exchange for hostages essentially has supplied and fueled their army. Nobody's tax money should be going to the Taliban.

And these dangers are more than mere hypothetical scenarios. Right now, as *The Guardian* reports, Germany is currently considering ending its policy of paying ransoms because of these exact concerns. Especially disturbing to them is the prospect that these ransom payments ultimately amount to "money which is eventually used to buy weapons which are used to kill our soldiers in Afghanistan." While Germany is beginning to learn their lesson the hard way, the government of Afghanistan has already wised up against the tactics of the Taliban. According to [Arabic television network] Al-Jazeera, the Afghan government refuses to exchange Taliban prisoners for hostages, citing the fact that they do not want to encourage more hostage-taking in the future.

Negotiation Encourages Kidnapping

Furthermore, while al Qaeda has long relied on hostage-taking, this tactic can quickly spread to others. Often home-grown terrorist cells or insurgents in Iraq will adapt the tactics of al Qaeda. In fact, the *Christian Science Monitor* reports that the Taliban's shift to hostage-taking reflects the influence of al Qaeda. Furthermore, some insurgent groups in Iraq as well as less radical organizations probably are on the border on deciding whether or not to kidnap innocent civilians. But if hostage-taking can prove to be a viable strategy, they have to reconsider. Ultimately, to stop the spread of hostage-taking to other, less radical organizations, as well as the extremely radical ones which already exist, the world has to send a message that hostage-taking and coercion will not work. Those who oppose us can sense any weakness we have, and they will often exploit these weaknesses to their advantage so long as any nation will play by their rules.

Nobody who refuses to negotiate with the Taliban wants to see these hostages die. Nonetheless, they see the bigger picture in this entire situation. Although the policy of non-negotiation may unfortunately spell doom for the Christian missionaries, these hostages, unlike the Taliban prisoners they could be exchanged for, will not die with a bomb strapped to their chest in a crowded marketplace. And as blunt as that may sound, it may very well be the truth of the matter.

Periodical Bibliography

The following articles have been selected to supplement the diverse views presented in this chapter.

Michael J. Boyle — "The War on Terror in American Grand Strategy," *International Affairs*, March 2008.

Adam Fresco — "Intervention in the Community to Beat Home-Grown Terrorism," *Times* (London), March 21, 2008.

Peter Goldsmith — "UK Terrorism Legislation in an International Context," *RUSI Journal*, June 1, 2006.

Spencer S. Hsu and William Branigin — "Anti-Terrorism Efforts Hailed," *Washington Post*, March 7, 2008.

International Herald Tribune — "How to Fight Terrorism: Russia and the U.S.; Misusing the Military," March 14, 2007.

Charles Krauthammer — "The Truth About Torture: It's Time to Be Honest About Doing Terrible Things," *Weekly Standard*, December 5, 2005.

G.P.H. Kruys — "The Role of Intelligence in Countering Terrorism and Insurgency," *Strategic Review for Southern Africa*, May 1, 2007.

Eric Schmitt and Thom Shanker — "U.S. Adapts Cold-War Idea to Fight Terrorists," *New York Times*, March 18, 2008.

Keith Suter — "Terrorism and International Law," *Contemporary Review*, October 1, 2005.

Karin G. Tackaberry — "Time to Stand Up and Be Counted: The Need for the United Nations to Control International Terrorism," *Army Lawyer*, July 1, 2007.

Ismail Vadi — "Terrorism, Public Policy and Democracy in South Africa," *Strategic Review for Southern Africa*, May 1, 2007.

Anthony C. Zinni and Leighton W. Smith Jr. — "A Smarter Weapon," *USA Today*, March 27, 2008.

For Further Discussion

Chapter 1

1. You have read opposing viewpoints regarding whether terrorism is a serious threat. What data do each author rely upon in forming an opinion on this question?

2. What does it mean for terrorism to be a serious threat? Compare the probability of a terrorist attack and the potential consequences of a terrorist attack.

3. You have read two viewpoints on whether we are winning the war on terrorism. How does each author differently define "winning"?

4. After reading opposing viewpoints on whether we are winning or losing the war on terrorism, what is your opinion? Cite from the viewpoints in support of your answer.

Chapter 2

1. After reading opposing viewpoints on whether nuclear terrorism is a threat, how serious do you think is the threat of a terrorist nuclear attack? Give reasons for your answers, citing from the viewpoints.

2. From the point of view of a terrorist, what are the pros and cons of cyberterrorism?

3. If there were a cyberterror attack on the United States, what targets do you think the terrorists would choose? Give reasons for your answers, citing from the viewpoints.

4. After reading opposing viewpoints on the danger of bioterrorism, do you think it is a danger? Why or why not?

Chapter 3

1. What do you think motivates terrorists to engage in terrorism?Cite from the viewpoints in formulating your answer.

2. Regarding poverty and terrorism, do you think poverty or unequal distribution of wealth is important as a motivating factor? Give reasons for your answer.

3. If the lack of civil liberties motivates terrorists, why do you think that is so?

4. Do you think that Islamic fundamentalism, by its very nature, causes terrorism? Why or why not?

Chapter 4

1. After reading opposing viewpoints on the use of torture in fighting terrorism, do you think torture should be used? Why or why not?

2. Persons define torture in different ways. How would you define it?

3. After reading opposing viewpoints on whether the Iraq war helps or hurts the fight against terrorism, what is your opinion on this issue? Give reasons for your answer, citing from the viewpoints.

4. What, in your opinion, are the pros and cons of negotiating with terrorists? Which position do you favor, and why?

Organizations to Contact

The editors have compiled the following list of organizations concerned with the issues debated in this book. The descriptions are derived from materials provided by the organizations. All have publications or information available for interested readers. The list was compiled on the date of publication of the present volume; the information provided here may change. Readers need to remember that many organizations take several weeks or longer to respond to inquiries.

American Civil Liberties Union (ACLU)
125 Broad St., 18th Floor, New York, NY   10004-2400
(212) 549-2500
e-mail: aclu@aclu.org
Web site: www.aclu.org

The ACLU is a national organization that works to defend Americans' civil rights. The organization believes that some measures taken to fight terrorism infringe on civil liberties and are harmful to democracy. The ACLU's Web site has articles and other information on infringement of civil liberties as a result of the war on terrorism.

Brookings Institution
1775 Massachusetts Ave. NW, Washington, DC   20036-2188
(202) 797-6000
e-mail: brookinfo@brookings.edu
Web site: www.brookings.edu

The Brookings Institution is a private, nonprofit organization that conducts research on economics, education, foreign and domestic government policy, and the social sciences. It publishes the quarterly *Brookings Review* and many books through its publishing division, the Brookings Institution Press. A searchable database on the organization's Web site provides access to articles on terrorism.

Center for Strategic and International Studies (CSIS)
1800 K St. NW, Washington, DC   20006
(202) 887-0200 • fax: (202) 775-3199
Web site: www.csis.org

CSIS is a public policy research institution focusing on America's economic policy, national security, and foreign and domestic affairs. The center analyzes global crises and corresponding U.S. military policy. The organization's searchable Web site has articles and information on terrorism.

Council on Foreign Relations
58 East 68th St., New York, NY   10021
(212) 434-9400 • fax: (212) 434-9800
Web site: www.cfr.org

The Council on Foreign Relations is an independent, national membership organization and a nonpartisan center for scholars dedicated to producing and disseminating ideas so that its members, as well as policy makers, journalists, students, and interested citizens in the United States and other countries, can better understand foreign policy choices facing the United States and other governments. It publishes the periodical *Foreign Affairs* as well as a number of books and reports. Many articles on terrorism can be found on the organization's Web site.

The Heritage Foundation
214 Massachusetts Ave. NE, Washington, DC   20002-4999
(202) 546-4400 • fax: (202) 546-8328
e-mail: info@heritage.org
Web site: www.heritage.org

The Heritage Foundation is a conservative think tank that promotes public policy based on limited government and individual freedom. The organization's Web site has a searchable database that includes many articles about terrorism.

Homeland Security Policy Institute (HSPI)
2300 Eye St. NW, Suite 721, Washington, DC   20037
(202) 994-0986 • fax: (202) 994-2543
e-mail: hspi@gwu.edu
Web site: www.gwumc.edu/hspi/

The Homeland Security Policy Institute, housed within the George Washington University, is a nonpartisan "think and do" tank whose mission is to build bridges between theory and practice to advance homeland security through a multi- and interdisciplinary approach. By convening domestic and international policy makers and practitioners at all levels of government, the private sector, and academia, HSPI creates innovative strategies and solutions to current and future threats to the nation. The organization's Web site has insightful and timely articles on terrorism.

International Policy Institute for Counter-Terrorism (ICT)
PO Box 167, Herzlia   46150
    Israel
972-9-9527277 • fax: 972-9-9513073
e-mail: info@ict.org.il
Web site: www.ict.org.il

ICT is a research institute that develops public policy solutions to international terrorism. The organization's Web site has articles and information on terrorism, counterterrorism, and terrorist organizations.

INTERPOL
200, quai Charles de Gaulle, Lyon   69006
    France
fax: 33-0472447163
Web site: www.interpol.int

INTERPOL is the world's largest international police organization, with 186 member countries. Created in 1923, it facilitates cross-border police cooperation and supports and assists all organizations, authorities, and services whose mission is to prevent or combat international crime. The organization's Web site has information on terrorism that has international impact.

Middle East Research and Information Project (MERIP)
1500 Massachusetts Ave. NW, Suite 119
Washington, DC   20005
(202) 223-3677 • fax: (202) 223-3604
e-mail: ctoensing@merip.org
Web site: www.merip.org

MERIP believes that stereotypes and misconceptions have kept the United States and Europe from fully understanding the Middle East. MERIP publishes writings from authors in the Middle East, a quarterly magazine called *Middle East Report*, op-ed pieces, and articles providing analysis and commentary on issues related to terrorism.

U.S. Department of Homeland Security (DHS)
Washington, DC   20528
(202) 282-8000
Web site: www.dhs.gov/index.shtm

The U.S. Department of Homeland Security is the federal agency tasked to prepare, organize, and mobilize our nation to secure the homeland from terrorist attacks. DHS's Web site has extensive reports, articles, and information on terrorism, terrorism prevention and protection, travel security, and terrorism alerts, including a searchable database.

U.S. Department of State Office of the Coordinator for Counterterrorism
Office of Public Affairs, Washington, DC   20520
(202) 647-4000
Web site: www.state.gov/s/ct

The U.S. Department of State is a federal agency that advises the president on foreign policy matters. The Office of the Coordinator of Counterterrorism publishes the annual report

Patterns of Global Terrorism, a list of the most wanted terrorists, and fact sheets and press releases on terrorism issues. These and other resources related to terrorism can be found on the agency's Web site.

Washington Institute for Near East Policy
1828 L St. NW, Suite 1050, Washington, DC   20036
(202) 452-0650 • fax: (202) 223-5364
e-mail: info@washingtoninstitute.org
Web site: www.washingtoninstitute.org

The Washington Institute for Near East Policy is a nonprofit organization that researches and analyzes issues concerning the Middle East and U.S. policies toward the region. The organization's Web site has articles, reports, and information on terrorism and issues related to terrorism policy.

Bibliography of Books

Abdel Bari Atwan   *The Secret History of al Qaeda.* Berkeley and Los Angeles: University of California Press, 2006.

Daniel Benjamin   *The Next Attack: The Failure of the* and Steven Simon   *War on Terror and a Strategy for Getting It Right.* New York: Times Books, 2005.

Peter L. Bergen   *The Osama bin Laden I Know: An Oral History of al-Qaeda's Leader.* New York: Free Press, 2006.

Rodney P.   *September 11, 2001.* One Day in History: The Days That Changed the World series. New York: HarperCollins, 2007.

I.W. Charny   *Fighting Suicide Bombing: Proposal for a "Worldwide Campaign for Life".* Westport, CT: Praeger Security International, 2006.

David Cole and   *Less Safe, Less Free: Why America Is* Jules Lobel   *Losing the War on Terror.* New York: New Press, 2007.

Phillip Cole   *The Myth of Evil: Demonizing the Enemy.* Westport, CT: Praeger, 2006.

Cindy C. Combs   *Terrorism in the Twenty-first Century.* Upper Saddle River, NJ: Prentice Hall, 2006.

Damon DiMarco, ed.
Tower Stories: An Oral History of 9/11. Santa Monica, CA: Santa Monica Press, 2007.

David Farber, ed.
What They Think of Us: International Perceptions of the United States Since 9/11. Princeton, NJ: Princeton University Press, 2007.

Jeanne Guillemin
Biological Weapons: From the Invention of State-Sponsored Programs to Contemporary Bioterrorism. New York: Columbia University Press, 2005.

Mary R. Habeck
Knowing the Enemy: Jihadist Ideology and the War on Terror. New Haven, CT: Yale University Press, 2006.

Bruce Hoffman
Inside Terrorism. New York: Columbia University Press, 2006.

David Hunt
They Just Don't Get It: How Washington Is Still Compromising Your Safety—and What You Can Do About It. New York: Crown Forum, 2005.

Raymond Ibrahim, ed.
The Al Qaeda Reader. New York: Broadway Books, 2007.

Sid Jacobsen and Ernie Colon
The 9/11 Report: A Graphic Adaptation. New York: Hill and Wang, 2006.

Jameel Jaffer and Amrit Singh
Administration of Torture: A Documentary Record from Washington to Abu Ghraib and Beyond. New York: Columbia University Press, 2007.

Thomas H. Kean and Lee H. Hamilton
Without Precedent: The Inside Story of the 9/11 Commission. New York: Knopf, 2006.

Ronald Kessler
The Terrorist Watch: Inside the Desperate Race to Stop the Next Attack. New York: Crown Forum, 2007.

Alan B. Krueger
What Makes a Terrorist? Economics and the Roots of Terrorism: Lionel Robbins Lectures. Princeton, NJ: Princeton University Press, 2007.

Evelin Lindner
Making Enemies: Humiliation and International Conflict. Westport, CT: Praeger Security International, 2006.

Aftab Ahmad Malik, ed.
The State We Are In: Identity, Terror and the Law of Jihad. Bristol, UK: Amal Press, 2006.

Mahmood Mamdani
Good Muslim, Bad Muslim: America, the Cold War, and the Roots of Terror. New York: Pantheon, 2004.

Joseph T. McCann
Terrorism on American Soil: A Concise History of Plots and Perpetrators from the Famous to the Forgotten. Boulder, CO: Sentient, 2006.

Thomas R. Mockaitis
The "New" Terrorism: Myths and Reality. Westport, CT: Praeger Security International, 2006.

Fathali M. Moghaddam
From the Terrorists' Point of View: What They Experience and Why They Come to Destroy. Westport, CT: Praeger Security International, 2006.

National
Commission on
Terrorist Attacks
upon the United
States

*The 9/11 Commission Report: Final
Report of the National Commission on
Terrorist Attacks upon the United
States.* New York: Norton, 2004.

Michael G. Paul

*Pan Am 103 and State-Sponsored Ter-
rorism.* Milwaukee: World Almanac
Library, 2006.

Walid Phares

*Future Jihad: Terrorist Strategies
Against America.* New York: Palgrave
Macmillan, 2005.

Richard A. Posner

*Countering Terrorism: Blurred Focus,
Halting Steps.* Lanham, MD: Rowman
& Littlefield, 2007.

George Soros

*The Age of Fallibility: The Conse-
quences of the War on Terror.* New
York: Public Affairs, 2006.

Ron Suskind

*The One Percent Doctrine: Deep In-
side America's Pursuit of Its Enemies
Since 9/11.* New York: Simon &
Schuster, 2006.

Gabriel Weimann

*Terror on the Internet: The New
Arena, the New Challenges.* Washington, DC: U.S. Institute of Peace Press,
2006.

Lawrence Wright

*The Looming Tower: Al Qaeda and
the Road to 9/11.* New York: Knopf,
2006.

John Yoo

*War by Other Means: An Insider's
Account of the War on Terror.* New
York: Atlantic Monthly Press, 2006.

Index

A

Abdulla, Bilal, 136
Abizaid, John, 168
Abu Gheith, Suleiman, 79–81
Abu Ghraib prison, 154
Abu Jamous, Muhammad, 138
Afghanistan, 176
Airplane hijacking, 17, 24, 28, 35, 69, 73
al-Arian, Sami, 59–60
al-Gama'a al Islammiya. *See* The Islamic Group
al-Hussayen, Sami, 60
al-Maliki, Nouri, 166
al-Qaeda (terrorist group)
    Americans as target, 26, 79–80, 173–174
    unlikeliness of attacks by, 36, 49–51
    bioterrorism and, 114, 123
    as continued threat, 60, 79, 81, 174–175
    cyberterrorism by, 110–111
    damage by, 36, 44–47
    difficulties for, 45–46
    importance of Iraq to, 58, 165–168
    leadership issues with, 42, 46–48, 52, 173
    Muslims against, 47
    as nuclear terrorists, 87, 93–94
    overreaction to, 45
    in Pakistan, 54, 60, 181
    sleeper cells in, 59
    theological treatises of, 147
    torture of, by CIA, 154–155, 157
    war on terror and, 24–29, 43–44
    See also bin Laden, Osama; Iraq war; Jihad/Jihadism; September 11, 2001
al-Zawahiri, Ayman, 134, 165–166, 174, 177
Allison, Graham, 71–82, 84, 87–88, 90–93
Alternative approach to terrorism, 39–40, 60, 152
American Civil Liberties Union, 20–21
American Muslims, 19, 51–52
Anthrax attacks, 58, 121, 123
Anti-American campaign, 46, 64, 173–174, 177
Apocalyptic terrorists, 86
Arar, Maher, 55
Archetypal terrorists, 85–86
Army Defense Intelligence Agency, 136
Asha, Mohammed, 136
Ashcroft, John, 55–56
Ashqar, Abdelhaleem, 60
The Assassins (Shiite Muslim sect), 16
Athanason, John, 31
Aum Shinrikyo (terrorist group), 17, 86, 121, 123

B

Bagaric, Mirko, 153–157
Baker, Howard, 75
Bakier, Abdul Hameed, 69, 105